Student Resou

Lynne Blesz Vestal

Glen E. Paterson
Confederation College

Anne Johnston Munroe
Sheridan College

Alex Munroe
Wilfrid Laurier University

Health: The Basics
SECOND CANADIAN EDITION

Rebecca J. Donatelle
Oregon State University

Lorraine G. Davis
University of Oregon

Anne Johnston Munroe
Sheridan College

Alex Munroe
Wilfrid Laurier University

Toronto

ISBN 0-205-33189-0

Acquisitions Editor: Andy Wellner
Developmental Editor: Lisa Phillips
Production Editor: Avivah Wargon
Production Coordinator: Wendy Moran

1 2 3 4 5   05 04 03 02 01

Printed and bound in Canada

TABLE OF CONTENTS

PREFACE TO THE STUDENT

This **Student Resource Manual** was designed to facilitate your understanding of health. By working on each corresponding chapter in your textbook, you will become an active participant in the learning process. Active participation involves more than just attending the lectures and reading the textbook — it means that you ask questions, hypothesize, are skeptical of some reported results, doubt some of the research findings, discover how concepts of health apply specifically to your life, and develop new questions to ask until you realize that you have more questions than answers.

Engage yourself in this learning process! When you do, you will become a critical thinker of health. When using critical thinking, you should question every fact and challenge every assumption, always asking yourself, "Do I agree with what the author is saying?" Another aspect of critical thinking is applying concepts of health to your own life, always asking yourself, "How does this concept apply to me?"

The following is an explanation of the contents of the manual that correspond with the chapters of the Health: The Basics textbook:

Chapter Overview
The chapter overview serves as a useful comprehensive summary in your reading of the textbook.

Learning Objectives
Before you read each chapter, scan the objectives to see what you are going to read. After reading each chapter and working on the questions in the student resource manual, you should be able to answer each question.

Key Terms
The key terms provide a helpful preview of key terms to be addressed in the textbook. Writing a brief definition of each key term in your own words will help you remember important concepts.

Critical Thinking Exercises
This set of exercises requires you to apply your knowledge from the text to real-life or hypothetical situations.

Critical Thinking Activity
Each chapter includes a critical thinking activity. The purpose of the activity is to facilitate critical thinking, and to help you learn to become a critical evaluator of health.

General Review Questions
Short answer and multiple choice questions are provided to help you focus on key concepts and practice your test-taking skills. The inclusion of some extra challenge questions may require you to seek answers from resources outside your textbook. Answers are included at the end of the manual.

Language Enrichment Glossary
College students who speak English as a second language reviewed the textbook and circled words they did not understand. These words have been compiled and explained for each chapter, in order to assist those who may need special language assistance or who have difficulty with health vocabulary.

CHAPTER 1
<u>Promoting Healthy Behaviour Change</u>

Chapter Overview

Health is defined as the "dynamic, ever-changing process of trying to achieve your individual potential in the physical, social, emotional, intellectual, spiritual, and environmental dimensions." This definition of health proposes a positive view that focuses on our individual attempts to achieve optimum well-being within a realistic framework of our individual potential. Health can be described on a continuum from illness to optimum well-being.

Health promotion combines educational, organizational, policy, financial and environmental supports to help people identify and change negative health behaviours. The focus of prevention is on making positive changes now, and making the best health decisions to protect against potential illness and disease.

There are key differences in health status between men and women. For instance, although women have longer lifespans than do men, they don't necessarily have a better quality of life. Many diseases, such as osteoporosis, thyroid disease, and lupus are far more common in women than in men. The nature of illness continues to change as we enter into the new millennium. Infectious diseases of the past have been replaced by accidents and life style behaviours as the major causes of death.

Predisposing factors, enabling factors, and reinforcing factors influence whether or not behavioural change occurs. In addition, our beliefs and attitudes will significantly affect what we do. The health belief model and the theory of reasoned action are useful models for explaining why people behave in a particular way. According to the health belief model, when perceived severity, perceived susceptibility, and cues to action support a belief, change is likely to occur. The theory of reasoned action explains that behaviours result from our intentions to carry out a behaviour. The more consistent and powerful your attitudes about an action and the more you are influenced by others to take that action, the greater will be your stated intention to do so. In addition, significant others influence our health behaviours, both positively and negatively.

After you have analyzed influences on your current behaviour and all the factors that may influence the desired behaviour change, you must decide which technique for behaviour change will work best for you. Techniques include shaping, imagined rehearsal, modelling, situational inducement, reinforcement, and changing self-talk.

One method of modifying your behaviour is to conduct a self-assessment of the antecedents and consequences of a situation to help you look at the circumstances in which your behaviour occurs, and then analyze its components. Then, when you decide to change a behaviour, you will be faced with choices. By developing your decision-making skills, you increase your chances of making the choice you really want to make. Finally, set behaviour-change goals that are realistic for you.

Learning Objectives

1. Define health and wellness, and explain the interconnected roles of the physical, social, intellectual, emotional, environmental, and spiritual dimensions of health.

2. Discuss the health status of Canadians, the factors that contribute to health, and the importance of A New Perspective on the Health of Canadians in establishing national goals for promoting health and preventing premature death and disability.

3. Evaluate the role of gender in health status, health research, and health training.

4. Identify the leading causes of death and the lifestyle patterns associated with the reduction of risks.

5. Examine how predisposing factors, beliefs, attitudes, and significant others affect your behaviour changes.

6. Survey behaviour change techniques, and learn how to apply them to personal situations.

7. Apply decision-making techniques to behaviour changes.

Key Terms

Fill in a brief definition to help you remember these terms.

health _____

mortality _____

morbidity _____

wellness _____

health promotion _____

prevention _____

primary prevention _____

secondary prevention _____

tertiary prevention _____

belief _____

attitude _____

health belief model _____

theory of reasoned action _____

shaping _____

imagined rehearsal _____

modelling _____

situational inducement _____

positive reinforcement _____

Critical Thinking Exercises

1. Health is multidimensional. Using the following scenario, apply the dimensions of health to Heidi's different components of health: Heidi is a 34-year-old married female with two children. She is a partner in a law firm, specializing in environmental law and works approximately 70 hours per week. She has a medium frame and is physically fit. Heidi is extremely competitive, both in her personal life and her work life. She competes in running marathons five times a year and publishes several law articles annually. She adapts well to a variety of social situations but tends not to always interact well with co-workers, as she has a high need for control. She describes herself as private and rarely expresses her feelings, except in an aggressive manner at work. She is also quite active in a volunteer program that educates the public on environmental issues. She has recently become involved in a church to which her husband already belongs.

2. Identify at least 10 health promotion efforts available to you where you live. How does each program enhance the likelihood that, once a person decides to change a behaviour, conditions are optimal for his or her success?

3. Marcel is in his second year at university. He smokes two packs of cigarettes a day. He started smoking when he was fifteen. When his room-mate warned him of the hazards of smoking, Marcel replies, "I'm going to die somehow, so I might as well enjoy myself." Using the health belief model as framework for discussion, explain what factors Marcel must consider before he will stop smoking.

4. Identify ways in which your family, friends, and other people have influenced your health behaviours.

5. Explain how the technique of imagined rehearsal could help someone who is preparing to compete in a tennis match.

6. Explain the basic premise of rational-emotive therapy. Identify 5 statements of irrational self-talk and replace each with positive, rational statements.

Critical Thinking Activity: A Self-Assessment

Identify one health behaviour that you would like to change. Conduct your own self-assessment by monitoring the antecedents and consequences of your behaviour. Use the following guidelines to help you in your assessment.

<u>I choose to change the following health behaviour.</u>

_____

_____

<u>Antecedents</u>
(List the setting events for your behaviour that cue or stimulate you to act in certain ways, such as physical events, thoughts, emotions, inner self-talk, or other people)

Behaviour
(Identify the behaviour)

Consequences
(List the results of your behaviour that affect whether you will repeat it or not)

Questions for the Critical Thinker

Analyze the health behaviour that you want to change by noting the following characteristics:

1. Frequency (How often am I engaging in this behaviour? All of the time or only once in awhile?)

2. Duration (Have I been engaging in this behaviour for a long time? How long?)

3. Seriousness (What are the consequences of my behaviour for me? for others?)

4. Basis for Problem Behaviour (Is my behaviour based on facts or my own perceptions of the facts?)

5. Antecedents (What kind of situations trigger the behaviour? Do some settings or people bring out the behaviour more so than others? Why am I engaging in this behaviour?)

Next, *apply decision-making skills,* referred to as **DECIDE**, to situations in which you have to make a decision about the health behaviour you want to change. By practicing the decision-making skills before being in a situation in which you have to choose among alternatives, you increase your chances of making the choice you really want to make. Use the space below to practice your decision-making skills.

Decide in advance what the problem is.

Explore the alternatives.

Consider the consequences.

Identify your values.

Decide and take action.

Evaluate the consequences.

Finally, *list specific goals* for how you plan to go about making this behavioural change. Identify goals that are *realistic and workable* for you.

1. _____

2. _____

3. _____

4. _____

5. _____

4

General Review Questions

Short Answer

1. What are the major dimensions of health?

2. Define prevention and identify three levels of prevention.

3. Identify three factors that influence behaviour-change decisions and provide an example of each.

4. Distinguish between belief and attitude.

5. What factors must support a belief in order for a change to be likely to occur?

6. What are the key components to analyze when you want to change a behaviour?

Multiple Choice

1. Prior to the 1800s, poor health was often associated with:
   a. The lack of penicillin
   b. The lack of medical care
   c. Poor hygiene and unsanitary conditions
   d. Diseases of heart and circulatory system

2. Statistics that are used to measure death rates are called:
   a. Morbidity
   b. Mortality
   c. Wellness
   d. Health Evaluation

3. The leading cause of death for all 15 to 24 year olds in Canada is:
   a. Cancer
   b. Accidents and adverse effects
   c. Stroke
   d. Heart disease

4. The performance of tasks of everyday living such as bathing or walking up the stairs are called:
   a. Improved quality of life
   b. Physical health
   c. Health promotion behaviors
   d. Activities of Daily Living

5. An appraisal of the relationship between some object, action, or idea and some attribute of that object, action or idea, is called:
   a. An attitude
   b. A cue to action
   c. A predisposing factor
   d. A belief

6. Life experiences, knowledge, cultural and ethnic inheritance, and cultural beliefs and values are called:
   a. Predisposing factors
   b. Enabling factors
   c. Readiness factors
   d. Reinforcing factors

7. Attending a health education seminar to stop cigarette intake is an example of:
   a. Primary prevention
   b. Health promotion
   c. Secondary prevention
   d. Tertiary prevention

8. The number of existing cases of a disease or disability is called:
   a. Prevalence
   b. Incidence
   c. Health status
   d. Cumulative percentage

9. Reinforcers that include such things as loving looks, affectionate hugs, and praise are called:
   a. Consumable reinforcers
   b. Activity reinforcers
   c. Manipulative reinforcers
   d. Social reinforcers

10. The type of disease prevention that involves treatment and/or rehabilitation after the person is already sick and is typically offered by medical specialists is referred to as:
    a. Primary prevention
    b. Secondary prevention
    c. Tertiary prevention
    d. Disease prevention

11. Taking prevention steps that stop a health problem before it starts is called:
    a. Primary prevention
    b. Secondary prevention
    c. Wellness
    d. Health promotion

12. The state of being that precedes a behavioral change is called:
    a. Cue to action
    b. Readiness
    c. Values
    d. Locus of control

13. Using positive self-affirmations to promote positive self-esteem and behaviors is a form of:
    a. Thought stopping
    b. Cues to action
    c. Modeling
    d. Self-talk

14. The setting events for a behavior that cue or stimulate a person to act in certain ways are called:
    a. Antecedents
    b. Frequency of events
    c. Consequences
    d. Cues to action

15. Programs that combine educational, organizational, procedural, environmental and financial supports to help individuals and groups change negative health behaviors and promote positive change are called:
    a. Health promotion programs
    b. Wellness programs
    c. Prevention programs
    d. Prevalence

16. According to the Health Belief Model, the process in which a person takes into consideration the severity of potential medical and social consequences if a health problem were to develop or is left untreated is called:
    a. Perceived seriousness of the health problem
    b. Perceived susceptibility to the health problem
    c. Cue to action
    d. Sociopsychological variables

17. The key behaviors that will help people live longer include:
    a. Maintaining healthy eating habits
    b. Sleeping a minimum of seven hours
    c. Weight management
    d. All of the above

18. Our ability to think clearly, reason objectively, and use one's " brain power" effectively to meet life's challenges is defined as:
    a. Social health
    b. Intellectual health
    c. Emotional health
    d. Spiritual health

19. The number of new cases of a disease or disability is called:
    a. Prevalence
    b. Incidence
    c. Health status
    d. Cumulative percentage

20. An academically trained health educator who has passed a national competency examination for prevention/intervention programming is a:
   a. Primary prevention specialist
   b. Health promotion specialist
   c. Certified health education specialist
   d. Certified prevention specialist

21. The dimension of health that refers to the ability to have satisfying interpersonal relationships is called:
   a. Spiritual health
   b. Emotional health
   c. Social health
   d. Mental health

22. Which of the following is(are) reason(s) for the exclusion of women from clinical trials?
   a. Their childbearing potential
   b. Variations caused by women's menstrual cycles
   c. Women's physiology
   d. All of the above

23. The theory that proposes that our behaviors result from our intentions to perform actions is called:
   a. Social Learning Theory
   b. Modeling
   c. Cues to Action
   d. Theory of Reasoned Action

24. Which of the following is *not* a factor that influences behavior and behavior-change decisions?
   a. Circumstantial factors
   b. Enabling factors
   c. Reinforcing factors
   d. Predisposing factors

25. Spiritual health includes all of the following *except:*
   a. The belief in a supreme being
   b. A specified way of living as prescribed by a particular religion
   c. To experience love, joy, pain, sorrow, peace, contentment
   d. To have satisfying interpersonal relationships

26. Learning behaviors through careful observation of other people is called:
   a. Thought stopping
   b. Modeling
   c. Reinforcing factors
   d. Cues to action

27. You want to bicycle for exercise but do not have access to a bicycle. This is an example of:
   a. Predisposing factors
   b. Enabling factors
   c. Reinforcing factors
   d. Cues to action

28. A relatively stable set of beliefs, feelings, and behavioral tendencies in relation to something or someone is called:
   a. Belief
   b. Value
   c. Social environment
   d. Attitude

29. Delicious edibles such as candy, cookies, or gourmet meals are examples of:
   a. Consumable reinforcers
   b. Activity reinforcers
   c. Extrinsic rewards
   d. Manipulative reinforcers

30. A form of cognitive therapy that is based on the premise that there is a close connection between what people say to themselves and how they feel is:
   a. Theory of Reasoned Action
   b. Thought blocking
   c. Locus of Control
   d. Rational-Emotive Therapy

Language Enrichment Glossary

In addition to the words in the Key Terms list at the end of the chapter, students listed the following words as difficult to understand. Use the chapter Key Terms list, this list, your dictionary, and teachers and friends to learn the meaning of words you do not understand.

abnormal:	unusual
acknowledge:	recognize, accept
adherence to:	obedience to
advocate:	someone in favour of something
antecedents:	events occurring before
appraisal:	assessment
attributes:	characteristics
berate:	criticize
buffeted:	pushed back and forth roughly
checkup:	physical examination
chronic:	periodic, persistent, long-lasting
clinical trial:	research tests
cliches:	common sayings
cliques:	exclusive social groups
coaxed:	persuaded
cognitive procedures:	thought processes
complex:	complicated
conclude:	assume
condiments:	things to flavour food
conform:	fit with
congratulate:	compliment
consistent:	in agreement with
constitute:	are made up of
conveyed:	carried or taught
coping:	managing
couch potato:	one who sits a lot
couldn't care less:	don't care
criteria:	guidelines
criticism:	negative judgments
crunch:	decision point
cues:	reminders
deficient:	missing something
deserted:	left

determinant:	cause
devastated:	destroyed in large numbers
deviations:	moving away from
devising:	developing
dimension:	part
dimensions:	areas
drawn expression:	very tired appearance
dread:	anticipate with bad feelings
dweeb:	foolish person
dwell on:	think about often
dynamic:	changing
dysfunctional:	not working well
embellishments:	unneeded extra things
enabling:	making possible
enhance:	increase
entity:	something
external trappings:	decorations
extrapolate:	make assumptions from
factors:	causes
fat intake:	fatty food eaten
feeling component:	emotions
flung:	tossed
foolproof:	error-free
foster:	encourage
fundamental grounding:	basic teaching
gaps:	missing information
gender:	male or female
generalities:	broad statements
genetic predispositions:	inherited tendencies
genetic:	inherited through the genes
getting down and dirty:	saying bad things about someone
gorging yourself:	eating too much
gossiping:	talking about something
holistic:	looking at the whole
hygiene:	clean health practices
idle chatter:	casual talk
immunity:	protected from something
immunized:	vaccinated
indicators:	measurements
insignificant:	not important
instilled:	taught
interactions:	communication between people
irrational:	not logical
landmark:	point used as a basis for comparison
life expectancy:	number of years lived

life span:	length of life
lifestyle patterns:	ways of living
lousy:	bad
maintain currency:	stayed up-to-date
maximize:	greatest increase
monetary:	money
mounting:	increasing
non judgmental:	not critical
norms:	customs
optimal:	maximum
ostracism:	isolation
overkill:	too much
oversee:	supervise
perspective:	outlook
physiological:	physical
predisposing:	creating a tendency toward
preoccupied:	distracted by
prerequisite:	initial requirement
primary:	most important
priority areas:	things of importance
quality time:	well-used time
rational:	logical, sensible
reinforcing:	encouraging
sanitize:	clean
sautéed:	lightly fried
self-efficacy:	personal competence
sensory acuity:	sharpness of the senses
shovelling in:	eating large amounts rapidly
significant others:	close relationships
solely:	only
sound:	strong
spectrum:	range
stick to your limit:	avoid going beyond your maximum
structured to exert:	designed to apply
subtly:	not obviously, indirectly
susceptibility:	easy to become ill
trigger:	cause, stimulate
unconditional trust:	complete trust
variables:	various things
verbalize:	say
visualize:	imagine
vital statistic:	information about people
willpower:	strength of will
zeal:	eagerness
zealot:	extreme enthusiast

CHAPTER 2
Psychosocial Health:
Achieving Intellectual, Emotional, Social, and Spiritual Wellness

Chapter Overview

Psychosocial health consists of intellectual, emotional, social, and spiritual dimensions of health. Intellectual health refers to the "thinking" part of psychosocial health. It includes such intellectual processes as the ability to reason, remember, interpret, evaluate, and solve problems. Emotional health involves the "feeling," or subjective, side of psychosocial health. Emotions are intensified feelings or complex patterns of feelings that we experience every minute of the day. Emotions include loving, caring, hating, pain, despair, letting go, joy, anxiety, fear, frustration, and anger. Social health is the part of psychosocial health dealing with our interactions with others and our ability to adapt to social situations. Our social health is tied to strong social bonds and key social supports. Spiritual health refers to a belief in some unifying force that gives a sense of purpose or meaning to our lives or to a sense of belonging to a greater scheme of existence.

Our psychosocial health depends upon how we perceive our life's experiences. While some experiences are under our control, others are not. Many factors influence psychosocial health, including the family, the greater environment, internal factors (such as your hereditary traits and your physical health status), personality, and maturity.

Your well-being is largely determined by your ability to respond to life's challenges and can be defined by your level of self-fulfillment. Attaining self-fulfillment is a lifelong process that involves building self-esteem, understanding and controlling emotions, and learning to solve problems and make decisions. The relationships we had with our parents and family when we were children have much to do with our self-esteem. Self-esteem can be enhanced through finding a support group, completing required tasks, forming realistic expectations, taking time for you, maintaining physical health, and examining problems and seeking help. Some researchers believe that negative emotions can make people physically sick and positive emotions can boost people's immune systems. Although there is a large body of evidence pointing to at least a minor association between emotions and physical health, there is still no definitive proof of such a relationship.

However, maintaining an optimistic mindset is probably sound advice.

Psychosocial problems include depression, anxiety disorders (including phobias, panic attacks, and posttraumatic stress disorder), seasonal affective disorder, and schizophrenia. Suicide is a result of negative psychosocial reactions to life. Among the risk factors for suicide are a family history of suicide, previous suicide attempts, excessive drug and alcohol use, prolonged depression, financial difficulties, serious illness in the suicide contemplator or in his or her loved ones, and loss of a loved one through death or rejection. Most people who commit suicide signal their intentions. There are a number of actions to take to prevent a suicide attempt. Such people can often be helped.

The number of Canadians who are turning to mental health professionals for help with emotional problems is increasing. Several types of mental health professionals are available to help.

Learning Objectives

1. Define psychosocial health in terms of mental, emotional, social, and spiritual components, and identify the basic elements shared by psychosocially healthy people.

2. Identify the internal and external factors influencing psychosocial health.

3. Discuss the positive steps you can take to enhance your psychosocial health.

4. Identify and describe common psychosocial problems, and explain their causes and available treatments.

5. Illustrate the warning signs of suicide and what actions can be taken to help a suicidal individual.

6. Evaluate the role gender plays in diagnoses of mental health.

7. Identify the different types of mental health professionals and the most popular types of therapy.

Key Terms

Fill in a brief definition to help you remember these terms.

intellectual health _____

psychosocial health _____

emotional health _____

emotions _____

social bonds _____

social supports _____

prejudice _____

dysfunctional families _____

self-efficacy _____

personal control _____

learned helplessness _____

id _____

ego _____

superego _____

behavioural psychology _____

developmental psychology _____

humanistic psychology _____

self-esteem _____

endogenous depression _____

exogenous depression _____

obsessive-compulsive disorders _____

anxiety disorders _____

phobia _____

panic attack _____

seasonal affective disorder _____

schizophrenia _____

psychiatrist _____

psychoanalyst _____

psychologist _____

social worker _____

counsellor _____

therapy _____

behavioural therapy _____

cognitive therapy _____

family therapy _____

psychodynamic therapy _____

posttraumatic stress disorder _____

Critical Thinking Exercises

1. As a residence hall director, Paul is concerned about the psychosocial health of the residents. You are the dean of the university's psychology department. Paul asks you to list the basic elements shared by psychologically healthy people. What do you tell him?

2. Suppose that your friend has had insomnia for the past month. She is about to turn to over-the-counter sleeping pills or tranquilizers to get some sleep. What methods can you suggest that would be less harmful?

3. Your friend tells you that he has been diagnosed with depression. He shares with you that he will be treated with a combination of cognitive therapy and interpersonal therapy. How are these two types of therapy similar? How do they differ?

4. Suppose you observe that your friend has withdrawn from her family and friends and from activities she once enjoyed. She has lost interest in classes and has been depressed following the breakup of a long relationship. She confides to you that she "can't take it" and says that she "might as well end it all." You are concerned that she might attempt suicide. What actions can you take to prevent a suicide attempt?

5. Yuri, your business partner, is reluctant to seek professional help for his emotional problems. He asks you for your advice. When you assess Yuri's need for professional help, what symptoms do you look for?

6. Your friend, Maria, tells you that she has scheduled her first trip to a therapist. She seems to have misconceptions about what therapy is and how it works. What can you tell Maria to expect in the therapy sessions and how she can get the most out of therapy?

Critical Thinking Activity: Constructing a Hierarchy Of Needs

Construct your own hierarchy of needs in the pyramid below. Fill in each need with your own examples of needs that you have already fulfilled, as well as those needs that you have yet to fulfill.

Questions for the Critical Thinker

After you have completed your hierarchy, reflect on the following questions. Your thoughtful responses will enhance your learning of this activity as well as your understanding of psychosocial health.

1. Psychosocial health involves the development and interaction of intellectual, emotional, social, and spiritual components. How do Maslow's needs apply to this definition?

2. Review the basic elements shared by psychosocially healthy people. What elements do you possess? For those you don't, how does Maslow's hierarchy have anything to do with it?

3. What does self-actualization mean to you?

General Review Questions

Short Answer

1. Identify four basic types of emotions.
2. What are the major elements shared by psychologically healthy people?
3. Describe the characteristics of a dysfunctional family.
4. What internal factors shape psychological well-being?
5. List the risk factors for suicide.
6. What are ways to develop and maintain self-esteem?
7. Name three major types of anxiety disorders.

Multiple Choice

1. The " feeling" part of psychosocial health that includes your emotional reactions to life is called:
   a. Emotional health
   b. Social health
   c. Spiritual health
   d. Self-esteem

2. A mentally healthy student who receives a D on an exam may be very disappointed by their grade and will:
   a. Reassess his or her course options and withdraw from the course
   b. Try to assess the reasons why s/he did poorly
   c. Make an appointment with the teacher to re-evaluate the test results
   d. Become cynical about passing the class and stop trying to get an A

3. Belief in some unifying force that gives a sense of purpose or meaning to life is called:
   a. Mental health
   b. Psychological health
   c. Spiritual health
   d. Egocentric health

4. Strong social bonds function to:
   a. Provide intimacy
   b. Provide opportunities for giving or receiving nurturance
   c. Provide reassurance of one's worth
   d. All of the above

5. A complex interaction of one's mental, social, emotional, and spiritual health is known as:
   a. Wellness
   b. Psychosocial health
   c. Health promotion
   d. Psychosocial prevention

6. A psychologically unhealthy person is characterized by all of the following except:
   a. Laughs, usually at others
   b. High energy, resilient, and enjoys challenges
   c. Has little fun, no time for him- or herself
   d. Has serious bouts of depression

7. A negative evaluation of an entire group of people that is typically based on unfavorable ideas about the group is called:
   a. Personal control
   b. Prejudice
   c. Phobia
   d. Learned helplessness

8. Our family, the greater environment, and social supports/social bonds are examples of:
   a. Internal factors
   b. External factors
   c. Intrinsic factors
   d. Self-efficacy

9. Marty flunked a math class two times and does not believe that he is good at math. He has resolved himself to not being able to graduate because he will never pass a required math class. This is known as:
   a. Learned helplessness
   b. External locus of control
   c. Seasonal affective disorder
   d. Post-traumatic shock syndrome

10. Anxiety disorders are characterized by:
    a. Fatigue
    b. Back pain
    c. Fear of losing control
    d. All of the above

11. To overcome the effects of insomnia, a person can use which of the following methods?
    a. Don't drink alcohol or smoke before bedtime
    b. Read, listen to music, watch TV, or take a warm bath
    c. Avoid reproaching yourself
    d. All of the above

12. Anxiety disorders that result from experiencing such traumatic events as rape, assault, war, or airplane crashes is called:
    a. Phobias
    b. Depression
    c. Panic attacks
    d. Posttraumatic Stress Disorder

13. After a shooting that left two students dead, the students at a local high school may experience:
    a. Posttraumatic stress disorder
    b. Depression

   c. Manic-depressive mood disorder
   d. Panic attack

14. A person with a Ph.D. degree and training in psychology, is called:
    a. A psychiatrist
    b. A psychologist
    c. A social worker
    d. A psychoanalyst

15. People suffering from schizophrenia may:
    a. Be unfailingly pleasant
    b. Be confused by multiple stimuli and respond inappropriately
    c. Have a clear sense of self
    d. Suffer from carbohydrate cravings

16. Susie is worried about the clothes she wears and says that she needs to buy a car that projects her as successful. What stage of Jung's View of Personal Growth and Spiritual Development is she experiencing?
    a. The dawn of life
    b. The morning of life
    c. The noon of life
    d. The evening of life

17. Sam is fatigued and is sleeping too much. He has no interest in hanging out with his friends or family. In addition, he no longer cares to snowboard or participate in other hobbies. Sam may be experiencing:
    a. Anxiety
    b. A phobia
    c. Depression
    d. Posttraumatic Stress Disorder

18. Disorders such as compulsions, phobias, and obsessive thinking are most responsive to:
    a. Behavioral and drug therapy
    b. Cognitive therapy
    c. Family therapy
    d. Psychodynamic therapy

19. Continual failure that causes people to give up and fail to take any action to help themselves is called:
    a. Learned helplessness
    b. Protective factors
    c. Learned failure
    d. Learned survival

20. The cause(s) of obsessive-compulsive disorders are:
    a. Low self-esteem
    b. Fear of losing control
    c. Alteration in a person's senses
    d. Difficult to isolate

21. One's sense of self-respect or self-confidence refers to:
    a. Self-esteem
    b. Social support
    c. Ego
    d. Developmental capabilities

22. All of the following are warnings of suicide except:
    a. A preoccupation with themes of death
    b. Increased interest in classes or work
    c. Failure to recover from a personal loss or crisis
    d. Giving away prized possessions

23. Depression that has a biochemical origin is known as:
    a. Manic-depressive mood disorder
    b. Exogenous depression
    c. Androgynous depression
    d. Endogenous depression

24. Which of the following is not true about phobias?
    a. They tend to be more prevalent in men than in women
    b. They are deep and persistent fears of specific objects, activities, or situations
    c. Simple phobias may be treated successfully with behavioral therapy
    d. Social phobias may require more extensive therapy

25. A psychological disorder among women that is characterized by depression, irritability, and other symptoms of increased stress is called:
    a. Depression
    b. Phobia
    c. Premenstrual syndrome depression
    d. Panic attack

26. A medical doctor who specializes in treating emotional disorders is:
    a. An Oncologist
    b. A Psychoanalyst
    c. A Psychologist
    d. A Psychiatrist

27. Therapy that aims to help a patient look at life rationally and to correct habitually pessimistic thought patterns is called:
    a. Family therapy
    b. Psychodynamic therapy
    c. Cognitive therapy
    d. Behavioral therapy

28. Suicide is more likely to occur:
    a. among college students
    b. among high school dropouts
    c. among high school students
    d. among middle age males

29. Panic attacks are caused by:
    a. Previously experienced trauma
    b. No obvious link to environmental stimuli
    c. Learned responses to environmental stimuli
    d. Both b and c

30. The type of phobia that occurs spontaneously and has no obvious link to environmental stimuli is called:
    a. Triskaidekaphobia
    b. Simple phobia
    c. Claustrophobia
    d. Agoraphobia

Language Enrichment Glossary

In addition to the words in the Key Terms list at the end of the chapter, students listed the following words as difficult to understand. Use the chapter Key Terms list, this list, your dictionary, and teachers and friends to learn the meaning of words you do not understand.

absessed:	enclosed, infected area
accreditation:	licensing
acknowledge:	admit to
adhere:	stick to
adjuncts:	additions
affiliated:	associated with, accompanying
afflicted:	affected by, bothered by
agonizing:	highly painful
alleviate:	lessen, relieve
alterations:	changes from original
apathy:	indifference, passivity, low energy
apparent:	appear to be; look as if
assess:	examine and understand
bewilderment:	confusion
black holes:	slang for deep emotional depression
bombarded:	being hit frequently by something
borderline:	on the edge of something
brags:	speak with pride about oneself
carbohydrate craving:	strong desire for carbohydrates
chaos:	disorder, unpredictability
cherish:	value something greatly
conclusive:	certain, convincing
contemplator:	thinker
correlates:	accompanies
credentials:	certificates, qualifications
criterion:	requirement, guidelines
curb:	limit
cynical:	distrusting, expecting the worst
debilitating:	weakening, crippling
despondency:	sadness, hopelessness
deteriorate:	break down
devastated:	destroyed
diagnosed:	found the cause for
dietary deprivation:	inadequate food or vitamins
diminish:	make smaller
discord:	disagreement
distorted:	unrealistic, not accurate
emerge from:	come out of
encompasses:	includes, surrounds
entails:	requires
epidemic proportions:	large numbers
execute:	do something
exerted:	effort towards, attempted

18

fallacies:	false, incorrect beliefs
fidelity:	faithfulness
flaw:	error
fluctuations:	moving up and down
fosters:	develops
gauge:	measure
gender bias:	prejudice against one gender
get your act together:	behave sensibly, responsibly
gratification:	satisfaction
grumpy:	irritable, bad tempered
habitually:	done regularly without thinking
hallmark:	measure of symptom of
hallucinations:	seeing things which are not real
heart palpitations:	not regular heart beats
hereditary:	inherited
immediate gratification:	prompt satisfaction of desire
immediate concern:	more important worry
impulses:	urges
in conjunction:	together
incremental:	small steps toward something
inherently:	basically, automatically
innate:	inborn, inherited
integral:	a central part of, indispensable
integration:	being involved with, connected to
interfering:	interrupting, getting in the way of
interpretations:	explanations
intertwined:	involved, wrapped around each other
intervention:	attempt to stop something
intricately:	delicately, in a complicated way
introverted:	loner; focussed on oneself
lethargy:	lack of energy, passivity
life span:	expected years to live
lingering:	continuing
linkages:	connections
lounging:	relaxing
lull:	calm, soothe
manifestations:	appearances
menopause:	when menstrual cycles end in mid-life
metropolitan:	associated with a city
mimic:	imitate
mind reader:	someone who can see into another's mind
mood elevation:	increased good feelings
nurturance:	care and nourishment
onset:	beginning
optimal:	best, highest
outlook:	expectation, point of view
outward:	external
overwrought:	extremely distressed
persistent:	stubborn, doesn't stop

pervasive:	widespread
phenomenon:	event, occurrence
ponder:	think, wonder about something
precepts:	basic principles, beliefs
precursor:	occurs before
predisposition:	tendency
premenstrual:	before a menstrual period
presumption:	assumption, expectation
prevalence:	frequent existence
provisional:	temporary until it can be confirmed
provoke:	cause something
rampant:	frequent and widespread
reason:	think something through
recurring:	happening over and over
reflection:	evidence of something
refrain from:	avoid
regressing:	going backward
reimbursement:	repayment
reinvigorate:	restore energy
resiliency:	ability to bounce back, recover
restrain:	limit, hold back
sap:	drain, wear out
scheme:	plan
sedated:	given drugs to calm
self-mutilation:	injuring oneself
set hierarchical order:	fixed pattern of importance
setback:	a reverse in one's progress
shelter:	housing, protection from the outdoors
sizing up:	estimating
snap out of:	leave suddenly
sort through:	examine one by one
static:	not changing
stifle:	limit, smother
stigma:	mark of shame
subtly:	not obviously, indirectly
suicide-prone:	likely to commit suicide
summon up:	gather together
superficial:	on the surface, not deep
surmised:	believed, assumed
take in stride:	handle or accept without problems
trampled upon:	treated without respect
traumas:	shocks, injuries
utterly:	completely
vicious circle:	a negative thing causing another
vital:	important
volatile mood swing:	rapid change from one emotion to another
ward off:	avoid, stop
zest:	enthusiasm, energy

CHAPTER 3
Managing Stress: Toward Prevention and Control

Chapter Overview

Stress is defined as our mental and physical responses to change. Positive stress, or eustress, presents the opportunity for personal growth and satisfaction, whereas negative stress, or distress, results in debilitative stress and strain. Although stress is inevitable, we can learn to recognize what causes distress and to anticipate our reactions. We can develop stress management techniques.

The three phases of the general adaptation syndrome describe the physiological response to stress. In the alarm phase, homeostasis is disturbed and the brain prepares the body either to fight or to run away (flight). In the resistance phase, the body has reacted to the stressor and begins to allow the system to return to normal. In the exhaustion phase, the physical and psychological energy used to fight the stressors has been depleted and illness may result.

There are three major sources of stress. These sources include psychosocial factors, such as changes, hassles, pressure, inconsistent goals and behaviours, conflict, overload, and burnout; environmental stress, such as natural disasters and background distressors; and self-imposed stress. Self-esteem, personality type and hardiness, self-efficacy, and control influence our ability to cope successfully with stressful situations.

University and college students experience numerous distressors, not just those related to academic achievement. Some symptoms of stress overload include difficulty concentrating on and finishing tasks, frequent mood changes, lethargy due to lack of sleep or excessive frustration, and disinterest in social activities. It is important to act promptly to reduce their impact. Most universities and colleges offer stress management workshops through their health centres or student counselling departments.

Stress management consists primarily of finding balance in our lives. In striving for this balance, we make the choice to react constructively to our stressors. Steps of stress management include examining any problem involving stress, assessing your stressors, changing your responses, and learning to cope. Stress management skills involve managing emotional responses, learning intellectual coping strategies, using physical activity to alleviate stress, managing your time, and making the most of support groups.

Learning Objectives

1. Define stress and examine how stress may have direct and indirect effects on your immune system and on your overall health status.
2. Explain the three phases of the general adaptation syndrome and describe what happens physiologically when you perceive a threat.
3. Discuss psychosocial, environmental, and self-imposed sources of stress.
4. Examine how evolving societal expectations may cause new kinds of stress.
5. Examine the special stressors that affect college students.
6. Explore techniques for managing stress.

Key Terms

Fill in a brief description to help you remember these terms.

stress _____

stressor _____
_____

adjustment _____

strain _____

eustress _____

distress_____

psychoneuroimmunology (PNI) _____

homeostasis _____

adaptive response _____

general adaptation syndrome (GAS)_____

autonomic nervous system (ANS) _____

sympathetic nervous system _____

parasympathetic nervous system_____

hypothalamus _____

epinephrine _____

adrenocorticotropic hormone (ACTH) _____

cortisone _____

conflict _____

overload_____

burnout _____

background distressors _____

cognitive stress system _____

psychological hardiness _____

hypnosis_____

meditation _____

biofeedback_____

Critical Thinking Exercises

1. What ways can you replenish your superficial adaptation energy stores, thereby conserving your deep stores?

2. Ellen's roommate habitually wakes her up in the middle of the night when she arrives home from parties. How can Ellen express her anger toward her roommate constructively?

3. Reframing, or changing the way you think, is a key element of stress management. Identify ways to reframe and provide personal examples of each reframe when applicable.

4. Reginald is preparing for his bar exam to practice law, and as a consequence, he is experiencing a great deal of distress. As a single father, he is struggling to balance the demands of studying and family obligations. How can he manage his time most effectively?

5. Who forms your support group? If you do not have a close support group, to whom can you go when you feel overwhelmed?

Critical Thinking Activity: Stress and the Student

University and college students face a number of stressful situations, such as homesickness, financial worries, academic achievement, and relationship problems. What may be a form of eustress to one student may be a source of distress to another. The purpose of this activity is to explore with other students what is considered stressful and to share ideas for managing particular stressors.

Complete the survey on university and college-related stressors. Then, select five volunteers from your class to take the survey. All volunteers need to be students. Provide a copy of the survey to each volunteer and ask them to complete the survey individually. Then have a group discussion on ways to manage stress as a student.

Survey of Student Related Stressors

Rank these common sources of student related stressors from 1 to 12, with I being the most stressful for you and 12 being the least stressful.

____ completing homework assignment

____ taking an exam

____ financial difficulties

_____ roommate problems

_____ making friends

_____ homesickness

_____ going on a date

_____ answering a question in class

_____ finding a part-time job

_____ keeping up your grades

_____ deciding on your major

_____ peer pressure

Questions for the Critical Thinker

After you have completed the survey, reflect on the following questions. Your thoughtful responses will enhance your learning of this activity as well as your understanding of managing stress.

1. How did your rankings of stress-related events compare with others?

2. Successfully meeting the stressful tasks related to university and college is a form of growth-producing eustress. Identify such tasks that have been a form of eustress for you.

3. Both eustress and distress have many sources, including psychosocial factors, environmental stressors, and self-imposed stress. Identify personal sources of stress related to attending university or college.

4. What causes the most stress in your life? What in your own behaviour increases your stress? What do you do to relieve the stress?

5. What components of stress management can help you achieve balance as a student?

General Review Questions

Short Answer

1. What are the phrases of the general adaptation syndrome?

2. Distinguish between eustress and distress, and provide an example of each.

3. What are the charcterisitcs of a Type A personality?

4. Describe the characteristics of psychological hardiness.

5. Describe stress inoculation.

1. The sudden burst of energy and strength that is believed to be one of our most basic, innate survival instincts is called:
   a. Eustress
   b. Adjustment
   c. Strain
   d. The fight-or-flight response

2. Stress that presents positive opportunities for personal growth are called:
   a. Homeostasis
   b. Strain
   c. Eustress
   d. Distress

3. The branch of the Autonomic Nervous System that is responsible for energizing the body for either fight or flight and triggering many other stress responses is:
   a. The central nervous system
   b. The parasympathetic nervous system
   c. The sympathetic nervous system
   d. The endocrine system

4. The hormone secreted by the adrenal glands that is responsible for stimulating the body is:
   a. Epinephrine
   b. Adrenocorticotropic Hormones (ACTH)
   c. Adrenaline
   d. Both a and c

5. The key region of the brain responsible for controlling the sympathetic nervous system and directing the stress response is:
   a. The pituitary gland
   b. The hypothalamus
   c. The adrenal glands
   d. The adrenal cortex

6. The phase of the General Adaptation Syndrome in which the physical and psychological energy used to fight the stressors have been depleted is called:
   a. Alarm phase
   b. Resistance phase
   c. Endurance phase
   d. Exhaustion phase

7. Conflict occurs when:
   a. We are forced to face two incompatible demands, opportunities, needs, or goals
   b. We are forced to speed up, intensify or shift the direction of our performance
   c. We must make adjustments to change
   d. None of the above

8. The wear and tear that our bodies and minds sustain during the process of adjusting to or resisting a stressor is called:
   a. Strain
   b. Eustress
   c. Stress
   d. Resistance

9. Overload occurs when we suffer from:
   a. Excessive time pressure
   b. Excessive responsibility
   c. Lack of support
   d. All of the above

10. Type C personalities:
    a. Thrive in stress-filled environments
    b. Succeed more often than Type A
    c. Have better health while displaying negative Type A patterns
    d. All of the above

11. During the Alarm phase of the General Adaptation Syndrome:
    a. The stressor disturbs homeostasis
    b. The body reacts to the stressor and adjusts to allow the system to return to homeostasis
    c. The body's adaptation energy stores release cells for energy and renew the energy reserves
    d. The energy stores are depleted and the organism dies

12. Mood-elevating, pain-killing chemicals that have a morphine-like action on the body and are produced by exercise are called:
    a. Endorphins
    b. Adrenaline
    c. Cortisol
    d. Norepinephrine

13. Symptoms of stress overload among college students include(s) all of the following, except:
    a. Prone to accidents
    b. Lethargy caused by lack of sleep or excessive frustration
    c. Increased ability to keep up with classes or concentrate on and finish tasks
    d. Frequent mood changes or overreaction to minor problems

14. The ability of the immune system to respond to assaults is called:
    a. Psychoneuroimmunology
    b. Adaptation
    c. Resistance
    d. Immunocompetence

15. According to Eliot, to reduce stress you should:
    a. Don't sweat the small stuff
    b. Remember that it's all small stuff
    c. Stress is only temporary
    d. Both a and b

16. The adaptive response to stress occurs when:
    a. The body attempts to return to homeostasis
    b. The stressor is no longer present
    c. There is a sense of relief that survival has been achieved
    d. Resistance to the stress has adjusted to a positive result

17. Events that can result in debilitative stress or strain are known as:
    a. Strain
    b. Stress
    c. Distress
    d. Adjustment

18. A balanced physical state in which all of the body's systems function smoothly results in:
    a. Homeostasis
    b. Distress
    c. Eustress
    d. General Adaptation Syndrome

19. The pituitary hormone that signals the adrenal glands to release cortisol is:
    a. Epinephrine
    b. Adrenocorticotropic hormone
    c. Endorphin
    d. Adrenaline

20. Feeling forced to speed up, intensify, or shift the direction of your behavior to meet a higher standard of performance, can result in:
    a. Hassles
    b. Pressure
    c. Change
    d. Conflict

21. A state of physical and mental exhaustion caused by excessive stress is called:
    a. Conflict
    b. Overload
    c. Hassles
    d. Burnout

22. There is evidence that suggests a strong relationship between excessive exposure to stress and:
    a. Depression
    b. Drug abuse
    c. Self-esteem
    d. All of the above

23. Rachel has just begun college and is having a hard time adjusting to her new demands. What types of chronic stressors can she expect as she continues in college?
a. Lack of privacy
b. Time management
c. Loneliness
d. All of the above

24. Overcrowding, discrimination, unemployment, inflation, and poverty are examples of:
a. Burnout
b. Conflict
c. Psychosocial stress
d. Background distressors

25. The part of the autonomic nervous system that functions to slow all the systems stimulated by the stress response is called the:
a. Parasympathetic nervous system
b. Sympathetic nervous system
c. Central nervous system
d. Cerebral cortex

26 Preliminary research data on stress levels and immune functioning supports that during periods of prolonged stress, elevated adrenal hormones:
a. Destroy or reduce the ability of natural killer T cells to aid the immune response
b. Improve the ability of natural killer-T cells to aid the immune response
c. Have no known affect on natural killer-T cells to aid the immune response
d. None of the above

27. Deep adaptive energy stores:
a. Seem to be influenced primarily by heredity
b. Release glycogen for energy in response to stressors
c. Store nutrients for the body's immune response
d. Are the resources that individuals possess to maintain the balance between their body and minds

28. A conscious attempt to simplify life in an effort to reduce the stresses and strains of modem living is called:
a. Adaptation
b. Conflict resolution
c. Burnout reduction
d. Downshifting

29. A stress management technique that involves self-monitoring by machine our physical responses to stress is:
a. Meditation
b. Biofeedback
c. Hypnosis
d. Deep-muscle relaxation

30. Losing your keys or having the grocery bag rip on the way to the door are examples of:
a. Pressure
b. Incongruent goals and behaviors
c. Hassles
d. Conflict

Language Enrichment Glossary

In addition to the words in the Key Terms list at the end of the chapter, students listed the following words as difficult to understand. Use the chapter Key Terms list, this list, your dictionary, and teachers and friends to learn the meaning of words you do not understand.

adversaries:	competitors, enemies
ailments:	illnesses
alleviate:	smooth
anonymity:	not being known
appraisal:	judgment
by-products:	things which result from
categorize:	place things in similar groups
circulatory:	blood system
circumstances:	characteristics of a situation
clergy:	ministers and priests
counterparts:	others that are similar
cramping:	painful muscle tightening
debilitative:	damaging, destructive
deviate:	change from
dilates:	expands
disgruntled:	annoyed, dissatisfied
disproportionately:	stronger than expected
dissipate:	lessen or eliminate
diverted:	turned away from
don't sweat the small stuff:	don't be bothered by small things
elicited:	brought up by
engendered:	caused by
equilibrium:	balance
exhaustion:	extreme tiredness
flexibility:	ability to adjust
fraternity/sorority:	academic clubs for males/females
fretting:	worrying
gimmicks:	tricks
hardiness:	strength
hostile:	angry toward others
impact:	influence of
impending:	upcoming, nearing
impetus:	motivation
imposed:	forced upon

inevitable:	cannot be avoided
inhibiting:	restricting, slowing
intangible:	doesn't exist physically
intolerant:	not willing to put up with something
legitimacy:	accuracy, correctness
locus:	place, centre
manifest:	appear
manifestation:	occurrence
mediating factors:	things which lessen a problem
migraines:	very strong headaches
modification:	change in something
onslaught:	attack
potential:	possible
prioritize:	rank in order of priority
proneness:	tendency toward
psyches:	minds, egos
replenish:	restore, refresh
replenish:	restore
reputable:	honourable, responsible
restorative:	creating health and well-being
rev up:	slang for increased speed of operation
self-imposed:	created by the self
speculate:	guess
stamina:	strength, ability to continue
status:	standing
stewing:	thinking often about something
strained:	difficult to maintain
stress-tabs:	vitamins to reduce the effects of stress
stuttering:	talk slowed by inability to pronounce words smoothly
susceptible:	sensitive to, easily affected by
sustain:	experience, suffer
switch:	replace with something else
tangible:	actual, physically exist
terminal:	deadly
theorize:	suggest, assume
thoroughly:	carefully and completely
thwarting:	preventing
untangle:	clarify
web:	net
weed out trivia:	eliminate unimportant things

CHAPTER 4
Violence and Abuse: Societal Challenges

Chapter Overview

The General Social Survey in 1987 estimated that only 31 percent of violent crimes are reported to police. In 1988, of 15 countries surveyed, Canada ranked fifth in victimization rates involving the use of force. The term violence refers to a subset of behaviours that produce injuries, as well as the outcomes of those behaviours. Several factors lead to violence and abuse, including poverty, unemployment, hopelessness, lack of education, cultural beliefs that objectify women and empower men to act as aggressors, lack of social support systems, and discrimination. By understanding the etiology of homicide, youth violence, bias and hate crimes, and violence on campus, you will reduce your own risk of becoming a victim and help ensure your own level of health. Homicide accounts for nearly 600 premature deaths every year, a steady decrease since 1975. Most homicides occur among people who know one another. As Canada becomes more diverse, there has been a corresponding rise in intolerance. It is believed that much of intolerance is caused by a fear of change and a desire to blame others when forces such as the economy and crime seem to be out of control. Youth violence occurs in both rural and suburban communities. Violence on campus seems to be fueled by alcohol abuse and other personal problems.

Domestic violence refers to the use of force to control and maintain power over another person in the home environment. It includes both actual harm as well as the threat of harm. As with homicide, the perpetrator is likely known to the victim. Women are even more likely to suffer violence from someone they know. Cycle of violence theories attempt to explain how women get caught in a downward spiral of domestic violence including abuse, contrition, further abuse, denial, and contrition that sometimes ends in deadly force. Child abuse includes sexual, psychological, or physical harm of a child by a caregiver. Spouse abuse is the single most identifiable risk factor for predicting child abuse. Most sexual abuse is committed in the home by a near relative.

Sexual violence against women continues to grow. A growing body of research shows that sexual assault is encouraged by the normal socialization processes that males experience daily. University and college students are particularly vulnerable to sexual assault (date rape). Certain social assumptions prevent the realization of the true nature of sexual assault by both the perpetrator and the wider public, including minimization, trivialization, blaming the victim, and "boys will be boys." Sexual harassment is defined as any form of unwanted sexual attention and this behaviour has become a concern in businesses, schools, and government.

Individuals can learn self-defense tactics that should lower a person's risk for assault. Prevention of violence begins with keeping yourself out of dangerous situations. There are several precautions you can take to lower your risk against rape, to prevent assaults at home, on the street, and in your car.

Learning Objectives

1. Discuss violence in Canada, including homicide, youth violence, bias and hate crimes, and campus violence.

2. Discuss domestic violence (abuse against women, children and men committed by their family members) and its causes.

3. Describe sexual victimization, including sexual assault, date rape, sexual harassment, and why it happens.

4. Identify the steps you can take to prevent personal assaults at home, on the street, or in your car.

Key Terms

Fill in a brief definition to help you remember these terms.

violence _____

homicide _____

domestic violence _____

child abuse _____

sexual abuse of children _____

sexual assault _____

sexual harassment _____

Critical Thinking Exercises

1. It is believed that much of intolerance stems from a fear of change and a desire to blame others when forces such as the economy and crime seem to be out of control. What can you do personally to prevent hate and bias crimes?

2. Suppose you are the director of a youth program based in a neighbourhood experiencing a lot of youth violence. What would you do to prevent young people from acting out violently?

3. Amanda was sexually harassed by her boss. When Amanda asked her boss a question about a report she was dictating, her boss commented on the size of her breasts. What actions should she take to prevent repeated sexual harassment and to help herself?

4. If a woman has just been the victim of a sexual assault, what should she do to help herself?

5. Kay is a single woman who has just moved into a new neighbourhood. What precautions should Kay take to avoid being assaulted in her home?

6. Cheryl is a first year university student who commutes 80 kilometres daily to attend classes. What steps can she take to prevent assaults in her car?

Critical Thinking Activity: The Impact of Television Violence

In this chapter, you learned about the growing epidemic of violence in this country. Violence is defined as a subset of behaviours that produce injuries, as well as the outcomes of those behaviours (the injuries themselves). Some have raised the issue of whether violence on television contributes to violence in society at large.

This activity is designed to help you determine the impact of television violence. Observe three 15-minute segments of the following types of television shows: a) cartoon show for children, b) news report, and c) a prime time show. As you watch each television segment, record the frequency, type, and duration of violent behaviours that you observe. After watching the segments, respond to the following critical thinking questions.

Questions for the Critical Thinker

After you have completed watching the television segments, reflect on the following questions. Your thoughtful responses will enhance your learning of this activity as well as the impact of television violence.

1. Compare and contrast each television segment on the frequency, type, and duration of violence observed.
2. Which television segment contained the greatest amount of violent acts?
3. Did these shows portray the consequences of the violent acts (e.g., people's grief over losing a loved one who had been murdered?)
4. At what age group were these shows aimed?
5. Could these shows have been told equally well without showing violence?
6. Why do you think people are drawn to viewing violence?
7. Do you think a prolonged diet of observing violent acts makes one desensitized to violence?
8. Should television violence be regulated by the government? If so, how?

General Review Questions

Short Answer

1. Explain Lenore Walker's cycle of violence and list the phases.
2. List five factors that increase the risk for violence and provide an example of each.
3. Identify four social assumptions that prevent the realization of the true nature of sexual assault by both the perpetrator and the wider public?
4. What causes young people to join gangs?
5. What preventative actions can be taken to ensure that sexual harassment will not be repeated?
6. List three factors that have been identified as risk factors for predicting child abuse.

Multiple Choice

1. A set of behaviors that produces injuries, regardless of whether they are intentional or unintentional is called:
   a. Aggression
   b. Accidents
   c. Abuse
   d. Violence

2. Which of the following is vulnerable to violence?
   a. Children
   b. Black males
   c. The elderly
   d. All of the above

3. The best way(s) to prevent a person from joining a gang is to:
   a. Keep that person connected to positive influences and programs
   b. Involve families, social service organizations, and law enforcement, school, and city officials
   c. Provide for programs staff who are well-trained, empathic, competent in dealing with emotionally charged issues, and understanding of the underlying factors that make youths chose the gang way of life
   d. All of the above

4. The threat of abuse and violence, including slapping, shoving, or breaking bones by someone in the home environment, is called:
   a. Rape
   b. Sexual assault
   c. Domestic assault
   d. Domestic violence

5. The single greatest cause of injury to women is:
   a. Auto accidents
   b. Rape
   c. Domestic violence
   d. Muggings

6. Child abusers tend to:
   a. Have been abused as a child
   b. Have feelings of isolation
   c. Have a tendency to abuse alcohol and/or drugs
   d. All of the above

7. The most frequent sexual abusers of children is (are):
   a. Parents
   b. Parents companions
   c. Spouses of the child's parent
   d. All of the above

8. All of the following statements about the impact of child abuse in later life are true, except:
   a. Ninety-nine percent of the inmates in the maximum security prison at San Quentin were either abused or raised in abusive households.
   b. Three hundred thousand children between the ages of 8 and 15 are living on the nation's streets and would rather prostitute themselves than return to abusive households.
   c. Most people who are abused as children do not end up as convicts or prostitutes.
   d. Male deviance or mental illness accounts for most incidents of sexual abuse among children.

9. Child abuse refers to the systematic harm of a child by a caregiver, generally a parent. This includes:
   a. Sexual harm
   b. Psychological harm
   c. Physical harm
   d. All of the above

10. Acquaintance or date rape is most common among:
    a. Minority high school females
    b. College women
    c. Mothers with small children
    d. Women in professional jobs

33

11. Rape by one person known to the victim and that does not involve a physical beating or use of a weapon is called:
   a. Simple assault
   b. Sexual assault
   c. Simple rape
   d. Aggravated rape

12. Much of the violence on college campuses is fueled by:
   a. Alcohol abuse
   b. Excessively high academic standards
   c. Personal problems
   d. Both a and c

13. Self-defense against rape should include:
   a. Learning self-defense techniques
   b. Taking reasonable precautions
   c. Developing the self-confidence and judgment to determine appropriate responses to different situations
   d. All of the above

14. Any act in which one person is sexually intimate with another without the other's consent is called:
   a. Sexual assault
   b. Sexual abuse
   c. Rape
   d. Sexual harassment

15. Injuries that occur without anyone planning or intending that harm occur are called:
   a. Assaults
   b. Intentional injuries
   c. Unintentional injuries
   d. Circumstantial injuries

16. Anger that is goal-directed, hostile self-assertion, and/or self-destructive in character is called:
   a. Violence
   b. Primary aggression
   c. Suicide
   d. Violence

17. For the average American, the lifetime probability of being murdered is:
   a. I in 450
   b. I in 153
   c. I in 28
   d. I in 3

18. Hate crimes tend to be characteristically:
   a. Excessively brutal
   b. Perpetrated at random on total strangers
   c. Perpetrated by multiple offenders
   d. All of the above

19. An abused wife will remain in an abusive relationship because:
   a. She is financially dependent on her partner
   b. She loves her partner and fears what will happen to him if she leaves
   c. Her cultural or religious beliefs prohibit her from leaving
   d. All of the above

20. Risk factors for gang membership include all of the following except:
   a. High self-esteem
   b. History of family violence
   c. Living in gang-controlled neighborhoods
   d. Academic problems

21. Susan was brutally murdered. The person most likely to have caused her death is:
   a. A stranger she met at the grocery store
   b. Her husband
   c. A man who was an ex-partner
   d. Most likely b or c

22. To reduce the risk of personal assaults while on the street, a person should:
   a. Walk with others
   b. At night, avoid dark parking lots, wooded areas, and any place that offers an assailant good cover
   c. Carry change to make a phone call
   d. All of the above

23. Injuries within the home typically occur in the form of:
    a. Falls
    b. Bums
    c. Intrusions by others
    d. All of the above

24. Which of the following is among the most dangerous occupations?
    a. Commercial fishing
    b. Bus drivers
    c. Postal workers
    d. School teachers

25. Based on research findings, men are more likely to commit sexual assaults:
    a. When attending large social gatherings
    b. During their senior year of high school or freshman year of college
    c. When they did not know the victim
    d. When their dates were dressed in a provocative manner

26. Why do people tend to be abusive in relationships?
    a. Alcohol abuse
    b. Marital dissatisfaction
    c. Dysfunctional communication patterns
    d. There is no single explanation

27. Rape that involves multiple attackers, strangers, weapons, or a physical beating is called:
    a. Sexual assault
    b. Simple rape
    c. Aggravated rape
    d. Simple assault

28. Which of the following is a common ploy by rapists to initiate their attacks?
    a. Requests for help
    b. Guilt
    c. Purposeful accident
    d. All of the above

29. Date rape is:
    a. A miscommunication between two individuals
    b. An act of violence
    c. A misperception on the part of males
    d. An inconsistent message that women give to men

30. Violence that is directed randomly at persons affiliated with a particular group is called:
    a. Physical abuse
    b. Psychological violence
    c. Social abuse
    d. Ethnoviolence

Language Enrichment Glossary

In addition to the words in the Key Terms list at the end of the chapter, students listed the following words as difficult to understand. Use the chapter Key Terms list, this list, your dictionary, and teachers and friends to learn the meaning of words you do not understand.

apt:	likely
boost:	lift
brutalized:	treated very roughly
callow:	immature
carjackings:	stealing someone's car while they're in it
coax:	persuade
coitus interruptus:	sex without orgasm

conviction:	belief
desecration:	dishonour
deviance:	abnormal, unhealthy
discern:	see
douche:	wash the vagina
dynamics:	interaction
empathic:	able to imagine how the other feels
etiology:	causes
flip on:	turn on
forestall:	prevent
foster:	encourage
hindsight:	making judgments afterwards
impunity:	without punishment
inculcation:	teaching
intent:	focused
interact:	be involved
intolerance:	prejudice
jocular:	funny
lurking:	hiding
mauled:	handled roughly
millennia:	thousands of years
minimization:	to make smaller
objectify:	seen as an object
odds:	chances
perpetrated:	caused
pervasive:	widespread
plagiarism:	taking credit for another's work
ploys:	tricks
precipitated:	caused
punitive:	harsh punishment
rash:	increased occurrence
relative:	in comparison
retaliation:	revenge
reverberate:	repeating sound
self-righteousness:	believing you are right
snuffed out:	killed
staggering:	unbalanced
stifle:	push down, to hold back
streaking:	running naked past a group
systematic:	repeated process
toxic:	poisonous
trivialization:	to make unimportant
variable:	characteristic
vigilant:	watchful

CHAPTER 5
Healthy Relationships and Sexuality: Making Commitments

Chapter Overview

Intimate relationships involve behavioral interdependence, need fulfilment, and emotional attachment. Each of these three characteristics may be related to interactions with family, close friends, and romantic relationships. Balanced intimacy requires developing levels of intimacy in several dimensions, including sexual, intellectual, emotional, aesthetic, recreational, work, crisis, commitment, spiritual, and creative intimacy. Balanced intimacy is a goal most people pursue either directly or indirectly. The chances for balanced intimacy are enhanced for people who were raised in an environment where close relationships were valued, and there were positive role models for friendships, close family bonds, and romantic attachments.

Despite dramatic changes in the family since the 1950s, all families still have in common the special bonding that a group of people with shared interests have for each other. Friendships are characterized by enjoyment, acceptance, trust, respect, mutual assistance, confiding, understanding, and spontaneity. Love relationships typically include all the characteristics of friendship, as well as fascination, exclusiveness, sexual desire, giving the utmost, and being an advocate. For Robert Sternberg, love is composed of three ingredients: intimacy, passion, and decision/commitment. According to Sternberg, the higher the levels of intimacy, passion, and commitment, the more likely a person is to be involved in a healthy, positive love relationship. Falling in love may be due to imprinting, attraction, attachment, and "cuddle chemicals."

Gender differences in relating styles stem from our social conditioning. Women are usually comfortable expressing highly personal thoughts to female and male intimates, while most men express their emotions to women rather than to other men. One theory is that men are less able to express emotions and achieve intimacy than are women owing to the process of identity development in infancy, considered more difficult for males than for females. The process of partner selection also shows distinctly different patterns. Factors that play a significant role in partner selection include proximity, similarities, reciprocity, and physical attraction. Men tend to select their partners primarily on the basis of youth and physical attractiveness, whereas women tend to place higher emphasis on partners who are somewhat older, have good financial prospects, and are dependable and industrious.

Obstacles to intimacy include lack of personal identity, emotional immaturity, and a poorly developed sense of responsibility. Barriers to intimacy stem from the different emotional development of men and women, an upbringing in a dysfunctional family, or other causes.

Commitment in a relationship means that there is an intent to act over time in a way that perpetuates the well-being of the other person, yourself, and the relationship. What separates committed from uncommitted relationships is the willingness of committed partners to dedicate themselves toward acquiring and using the skills that will ensure a lasting relationship. The major types of committed relationships are marriage, cohabitation, and gay and lesbian partnerships.

Success in committed relationships requires understanding the roles of partnering scripts. Accountability and self-nurturance are especially important in knowing yourself and maintaining a good relationship. People in healthy committed relationships trust one another, meaning there is predictability, dependability, and faith.

More people are remaining single, either by choice or by chance. Many single people live rich, rewarding lives and maintain a large network of close friends and families. Having children changes a couple's relationship. Resources of time, energy, and money are split many ways, and the partners no longer have each other's undivided attention. Consistency, communication, affection, and mutual respect are important to the well-being of the family unit.

Breakdowns in relationships usually start with a change in communication. Couples may seek help from private practitioners trained to counsel married or committed couples, community mental health centres, psychiatrists, licensed psychologists, social workers, or counsellors with advanced degrees. The decision to end a relationship is usually difficult, and it often takes at least a year or longer to recover from the loss of a major relationship. With time, support from others, and community or professional help, most people do recover and establish new relationships.

Your sexual identity is determined by a complex interaction of genetic, physiological, and environmental factors. Defining your sexual identity is a lifelong process of growing and learning. Your sexual identity is made up of the unique combination of your sex, gender identity, chosen gender roles, sexual preference, and personal experiences.

An understanding of the female and male reproductive systems will help you derive pleasure and satisfaction from your sexual relationships, be sensitive to your partner's wants and needs, and be more responsible about your choices regarding your own sexual health. The female reproductive system includes the mons pubis, the labia minora and majora, the clitoris, the urethral and vaginal openings, the vestibule of the vagina, vagina, uterus, fallopian tubes, and ovaries. The male reproductive system includes the penis, scrotum, testes, epididymides, vasa deferentia, urethra, the seminal vesicles, the prostrate gland, and the Cowper's glands.

For both males and females, the human sexual response is a physiological process that involves four stages: excitement/arousal, plateau, orgasm, and resolution. Some males experience a fifth stage, the refractory period. The response stages occur during masturbation, heterosexual activity, and homosexual activity. Sexual orientation refers to your preference for emotional, social, and sexual situations. Sexual orientation is often categorized by heterosexuality, homosexuality, and bisexuality. One's sexual orientation is most likely determined by a combination of biological and environmental factors that are unique to each person. The range of human sexual expression is broad, and therefore many sexual activities are considered "normal," such as celibacy, autoerotic behaviours, kissing and erotic touching, oral-genital stimulation, anal intercourse, and vaginal intercourse. Variant sexual behaviours are sexual behaviours that are not engaged in by most people, such as group sex and transvestitism.

Various problems associated with achieving sexual satisfaction are called sexual dysfunction. Sexual dysfunction can include sexual desire disorders, sexual arousal disorders, orgasm disorders, and sexual pain disorders. Use of various drugs can also lead to sexual dysfunction. Sexual dysfunction can usually be treated successfully with therapy.

Learning Objectives

1. Explain the characteristics of intimate relationships, the purposes they serve, and the types of intimacy that each of us may be able to have.

2. Explain how relationships develop, potential barriers to healthy relationships, and factors that are important in maintaining intimate relationships.

3. Discuss what role remaining single means for many Canadians.

4. Examine child-rearing practices in Canada and the importance of a healthy family environment.

5. Discuss the warning signs of relationship decline, where you can go to get help with a relationship crisis, and factors that ultimately lead to relationship problems.

6. Define sexual identity, and discuss the role of gender identity.

7. Identify the components of male and female reproductive anatomy and physiology and their functions.

8. Discuss the options available for the expression of one's sexuality.

9. Classify sexual dysfunction and describe each disorder.

10. Learn to develop your own sexual identity.

Key Terms

Fill in a brief definition to help you remember these terms.

intimate relationships _____

emotional availability _____

dysfunctional family _____

jealousy _____

monogamy _____

serial monogamy _____

open relationship _____

cohabitation _____

common-law marriage _____

accountability _____

self-nurturance _____

trust _____

power _____

autonomy _____

sexual identity _____

gonads _____

puberty _____

pituitary gland _____

secondary sex characteristics _____

gender roles _____

gender identity _____

gender role stereotypes _____

androgyny _____

socialization _____

external female genitals _____

vulva _____

mons pubis _____

labia minora _____

labia majora _____

clitoris _____

urethral opening _____

vagina _____

hymen _____

perineum _____

internal female genitals _____

uterus (womb) _____

endometrium _____

cervix _____

ovaries _____

fallopian tubes _____

puberty _____

pituitary gland _____

hypothalamus _____

gonadotropin-releasing hormone (GnRH) _____

follicle-stimulating hormone (FSH) _____

luteinizing hormone (LH) _____

estrogens _____

progesterone _____

menarche _____

ovarian follicles (egg sacs) _____

ovulation _____

human chorionic gonadotropin (HCG) _____

menopause _____

external male genitals _____

internal male genitals _____

accessory glands _____

penis _____

ejaculation _____

scrotum _____

testes _____

testosterone _____

spermatogenesis _____

epididymis _____

vas deferens _____

seminal vesicles _____

semen _____

prostate gland _____

foreskin _____

vasocongestion _____

sexual orientation _____

heterosexual _____

homosexual _____

bisexual _____

homophobia _____

limerance _____

celibacy _____

autoerotic behaviours _____

sexual fantasies _____

masturbation _____

erogenous zones _____

cunnilingus _____

fellatio _____

anal intercourse _____

vaginal intercourse _____

variant sexual behaviour _____

sexual dysfunction _____

inhibited sexual desire (ISD) _____

sexual aversion disorder _____

erectile dysfunction_____

impotence _____

premature ejaculation _____

retarded ejaculation_____

preorgasmic_____

dyspareunia _____

vaginismus_____

Critical Thinking Exercises

1. Jack and Sarah describe their relationship as one in which they feel very close to each other and have a romantic and sexual attraction for each other. However, they have not made any commitment to each other about their love. What type of relationship do they have?

2. Every time Ben and Susan go to a party, Ben gets extremely jealous when Susan talks to other men. What are some possible causes of Ben's jealousy?

3. What is a partnering script? What script were you raised with that influences what is expected of you as an adult? How does it influence your partner selection?

4. When Felipe explained to his parents that he trusts his fiancee, what does he mean?

5. Following her divorce from Andy, Sandy is experiencing great loneliness and an intense desire for new relationships. What steps can she take to cope effectively?

6   Recall your own childhood. How were gender roles shaped or socialized by your parents, other family members, peers, schools, textbooks, advertisements, television, music, and movies?

7. Match the following sexual dysfunctions with the descriptions that follow.

    a. inhibited sexual desire

    b. vaginismus

    c. dyspareunia

    d. premature ejaculation

    e. erectile dysfunction

    f. retarded ejaculation

    g. sexual aversion disorder

____ 1. When Lateefah was a child, she was sexually abused by her stepfather. As an adult, Lateefah experiences a great deal of anxiety about sexual contact.

____ 2. Janet is seeking out a sex therapist because she doesn't have any interest in sexual activity.

____ 3. Todd has an orgasm disorder in which he is unable to ejaculate once his penis is erect.

____ 4. Marco is experiencing difficulty in maintaining a penile erection for intercourse. His urologist asks him if he is still taking medication for high blood pressure.

___ 5. Anthony goes to his urologist for a physical examination and complains of ejaculating soon after the insertion of the penis into the vagina.

___ 6. Sarita has experienced pain during intercourse since she was diagnosed with endometriosis.

___ 7. Bev's gynecologist explained to her that her fear of intercourse is most likely contributing to the involuntary contraction of vaginal muscles, making penile insertion painful.

Critical Thinking Activity: Assessing Your Sexuality

In order to evaluate your attitudes toward sexuality, complete the following sentences.

1. My definition of masculinity is
2. My definition of femininity is
3. I think my body is
4. My sexual experiences have been
5. My parents' attitude toward sex
6. A healthy sexual relationship is
7. Homosexuality is
8. When it comes to talking about sex with my partner, I
9. Regarding male and female reproductive anatomy, my knowledge is
10. My feelings about variant sexual behaviours are

General Review Questions

Short Answer

1. What psychological needs do intimate relationships fulfil?
2. Describe the characteristics of love relationships.
3. Identify the three key ingredients of love as presented in Sternberg's Triangular Theory of Love.
4. Identify secondary sex characteristics in males and in females.
5. Identify stages in the sexual response cycle.
6. Explain the effect of alcohol on sexual performance.

Multiple Choice

1. Sexual identity is defined by a person's:
   a. Biological sex
   b. Gender identity
   c. Gender roles
   d. All of the above

2. Which of the following statements is true about androgyny?
   a. Androgyny is a combination of traditional masculine and feminine traits in a single person
   b. Androgyny is the personal sense or awareness of being either masculine or feminine
   c. Androgyny is the process by which a society transmits behavioral expectations to its individual members
   d. Androgyny is the generalized way in which males and females express themselves the characteristics of each process

3. All of the following are part of the vulva, except:
   a. Labia minora
   b. Glans clitoris
   c. Vagina
   d. Mons veneris

4. The ovaries:
   a. Contain tiny hair-like fibers called fimbriae
   b. Are the reservoir for immature eggs
   c. Are a hollow, muscular tube capable of expanding to accommodate the passage of an infant during birth
   d. Are the most common sites of fertilization

5. Ovulation usually occurs on the:
   a. Seventh day of the proliferatory phase
   b. Fourteenth day of the proliferatory phase
   c. Twenty-first day of the proliferatory phase
   d. Twenty-eighth day of the proliferatory phase

6. Menopause is the result of:
   a. An increase in the production of testosterone
   b. The presence of human chorionic gonadotropin
   c. A sudden and permanent release of epinephrine
   d. A decrease in estrogen levels

7. Testes are responsible for the manufacture of.
   a. Progestin
   b. Follicle stimulating hormone
   c. Testosterone
   d. Androgens

8. The structure where immature sperm ripen and reach full maturity is the:
   a. Testosterone
   b. Cowper's gland
   c. Vasa deferentia
   d. Epididymis

9. The organ that deposits sperm in the vagina is called:
   a. The testes
   b. The prostate gland
   c. The penis
   d. The ejaculatory organ

10. People who are emotionally and sexually attracted to members of both sexes are:
    a. Heterosexual
    b. Homosexual
    c. Bisexual
    d. Homogeneous

11. During the human sexual response, vasocongestion occurs in the _____ phase.
    a. Excitement/arousal
    b. Plateau
    c. Orgasm
    d. Resolution

45

12. The avoidance or abstention from sexual activities with others is called:
    a. Celibacy
    b. Homosexuality
    c. Limerence
    d. Autoerotic behaviors

13. A condition in which a person experiences sexual arousal by looking at or touching inanimate objects, such as underclothing or shoes, is called:
    a. Transvestitism
    b. Fetishism
    c. Voyeurism
    d. Sadomasochism

14. The most frequent problem that causes people to seek out a sex therapist is:
    a. Erectile dysfunction
    b. Inhibited sexual desire
    c. Premature ejaculation
    d. Dyspareunia

15. Ejaculation that occurs prior to or almost immediately following penile penetration of the vagina is called:
    a. Impotence
    b. Premature ejaculation
    c. Retarded ejaculation
    d. Erectile dysfunction

16. The differential development of male and female gonads occurs at about:
    a. The 8th week of fetal life
    b. The 20th week of fetal life
    c. The last trimester of fetal life
    d. The 2nd week after birth

17. A personal sense or awareness of being masculine or feminine is called:
    a. Androgyny
    b. Gender identity
    c. Gender roles
    d. Gender role stereotypes

18. The hollow, muscular tube through which menstrual flow leaves the female's body is:
    a. Fallopian tubes
    b. Vagina
    c. Uterus
    d. Cervix

19. The lower end of the uterus that opens into the vagina is called:
    a. The vagina
    b. The hymen
    c. The fallopian tubes
    d. The cervix

20. The hormone that signals the ovaries to begin producing estrogen is:
    a. Gonadotropin-releasing hormone
    b. Follicle-stimulating hormone
    c. Luteinizing hormone
    d. Human Chorionic Gonadotropin

21. The internal male genitals include all of the following except:
    a. Testes
    b. Scrotum
    c. Vasa deferentia
    d. Prostate

22. Homophobia is:
    a. The irrational hatred or fear of homosexuality in others
    b. The fear of homosexual feelings within one's self
    c. Self-loathing because of one's homosexuality
    d. All of the above

23. The oral stimulation of a male's genitals is called:
    a. Cunnilingus
    b. Fellatio
    c. Coitus
    d. Autoerotic behaviors

24. The exposure of one's genitals to strangers in public places is called:
   a. Pedophilia
   b. Exhibitionism
   c. Voyeurism
   d. Transsexualism

25. Difficulty in achieving or maintaining a penile erection sufficient for intercourse is called:
   a. Erectile dysfunction
   b. Premature ejaculation
   c. Inhibited sexual desire
   d. Performance anxiety

26. Sexual activities in which gratification is received by inflicting pain are called:
   a. Transvestitism
   b. Fetishism
   c. Pedophilia
   d. Sadomasochism

27. Which of the following theories best explains the origin of sexual orientation?
   a. Prenatal hormone levels and structural differences in the brain determines sexual orientation
   b. Environmental factors such as being sexually abused during childhood cause an individual to become homosexual
   c. Social and psychological factors such as an overbearing mother and passive father cause an individual to become homosexual
   d. The cause or causes of sexual orientation are complex and is best understood using a multi-factorial model which incorporates biological, socio-environmental, and psychological factors

28. Which of the following is(are) a common form of nonverbal sexual communication?
   a. Kissing
   b. Touching
   c. Sexual fantasies
   d. Both a and b

29. The most widely practiced form of sexual expression for most couples is:
   a. Cunnilingus
   b. Anal intercourse
   c. Vaginal intercourse
   d. Fellatio

30. The most common side effect(s) reported for Viagra is (are):
   a. Stomach ache
   b. Urinary tract infection
   c. Diarrhea
   d. All of the above

Language Enrichment Glossary

In addition to the words in the Key Terms list at the end of the chapter, students listed the following words as difficult to understand. Use the chapter Key Terms list, this list, your dictionary, and teachers and friends to learn the meaning of words you do not understand.

abdomen:	stomach area
abnormalities:	things which are not normal
abound:	exist in large numbers
acquaintances:	people not known well
agony:	pain
alimony:	support payments after divorce
alleviate:	reduce
anatomical:	related to the body structure
anesthetic:	drug to lessen pain
annoyance:	irritation
apparently:	likely, seems to
arena:	area, topic
aspects:	different sides to something
assume:	expect, take for granted
attributes:	characteristics
aversive:	strongly negative
child-rearing practices:	ways of raising children
cognitive:	related to thought
cornerstones:	foundations
corporate ladder:	levels of job status
coarse:	rough, not smooth
criteria:	measurement
cuddle:	hug, snuggle
delineated:	defined, outlined
designated:	specified
deviant:	different from normal
dwelling:	thinking often about something
dimensions:	areas
discernible:	separate, distinct
disparity:	contrast, difference
divulge:	to reveal, tell
ecstasy:	joy
elaboration:	giving more details
elation:	joy, delight
eliciting:	bringing up
equated:	associated with
equivalent:	the same as
erotic:	sexually stimulating
erroneously:	incorrectly
eternal quest:	never-ending search

evolve:	develop
exclusiveness:	limited to one person
fascination:	to have strong interest in
formation:	development
fraternal twins:	twins from separate eggs
frowns:	looks down upon; discourages
gratification:	satisfaction
grooming:	personal cleanliness
hampered:	frustrated, interfered with
hostility:	hate, anger
implantation:	act of inserting something
inanimate:	not alive
inclination:	tendency toward something
inhibits:	slows down, holds back
insemination:	to become pregnant
integration:	union with others
intertwined:	involved with each other
retrospection:	self-analysis
intrusive:	distracting, annoying
junkies:	people addicted to something
justified:	defended, excused
lesbians:	women sexually attracted to other women
love-smitten:	captivated by love
lubricate:	to become slippery
matrimony:	marriage
muttered:	spoken quietly
norm:	average
nurturing:	caring for
pathological:	disorder in behaviour, disease
penile:	related to the penis
perpetuates:	continues
precludes:	prevents
prenatal:	before birth
pristine:	perfect
provocative:	interesting, intriguing
provoke:	cause
proximity:	nearness
punctuated:	emphasized, highlighted
reciprocal:	mutual, shared
reciprocity:	return similar behaviour
refute:	contradict
resilient:	strong, flexible
rhythmic:	a recurring pattern
scripting:	habitual behaviour
secrete:	release

shed light:	reveal
sloughed off:	dropped off the top layer
soaring:	rising rapidly
solidify:	make stronger
sort out:	separate, place in order
speculate:	guess, imagine
spontaneity:	action without planning
spur:	cause, act as a stimulus
stem:	come from
stigma:	shame
succinctly:	briefly, directly
tactics:	strategies
theme:	focus, subject
traits:	characteristics
trigger mechanism:	something that causes something else
triggered:	caused
ultimately:	finally
unsolicited:	unasked
utmost:	maximum
verbalize:	say
vastly:	enormously
via:	by or through
vital:	necessary
void:	absence, empty space
wading:	moving slowly through something

CHAPTER 6
Birth Control, Pregnancy, and Childbirth: Managing Your Fertility

Chapter Overview

Conception refers to the fertilization of an ovum by a sperm. In order for conception to occur, there must be a viable egg, a viable sperm, and access to the egg by the sperm. Contraception refers to methods of preventing conception. Reversible methods of contraception include abstinence and "outercourse," the condom, oral contraceptives, progestin-only pills, the morning-after pill, foams, suppositories, jellies, creams, the female condom, the diaphragm with spermicidal jelly or cream, the contraceptive sponge, cervical cap, intrauterine devices, and withdrawal. New methods of birth control include Depo-Provera and Norplant. Researchers are working on new male contraceptives. Fertility awareness methods include the cervical mucous method, body temperature method, and the calendar method. Tubal ligation is a method of sterilization in females, and a procedure called a vasectomy is used for sterilization in males.

An abortion is the medical means of terminating a pregnancy. In 1869, a law was enacted prohibiting abortion. In 1967 the Federal Standing Committee on Health began studying proposed amendments to the Criminal Code relating to abortion. Only a few hospitals perform abortions; many are performed in clinics. Legally, abortion continues to be a grey area. The type of abortion procedure used is determined by the duration of the pregnancy.

The decision to become a parent involves a number of considerations, including your emotional health, maternal and paternal health, financial well-being, and contingency planning.

Good prenatal care is essential for a successful pregnancy. Regular medical checkups, beginning as early in the pregnancy as possible, are essential. Other factors that contribute to a successful pregnancy include the availability of skilled medical practitioners, the mother's avoidance of drugs and medication, her avoidance of X-rays, her physical condition, good nutrition and exercise, confidence in her ability to give birth, and her support system. Pregnancy typically lasts 40 weeks, and is divided into three trimesters, of approximately three months each. A number of prenatal testing and screening procedures are able to detect health defects in a fetus, including amniocentesis, ultrasound, fetoscopy, and chorionic villus sampling.

There are three stages in the birth process. In the first stage, the amniotic sac breaks, causing a rush of fluid from the vagina. Contractions push the baby downward, causing the cervix to dilate further. When the cervix is sufficiently dilated, the second stage begins. During expulsion, uterine contractions push the baby through the birth canal. Expulsion concludes when the infant is finally pushed out of the mother's body. The third stage, afterbirth, occurs when the placenta is expelled from the womb, usually within thirty minutes after delivery. Problems and complications can occur during labour and delivery, even following a successful pregnancy. Such possibilities should be discussed with the medical practitioner prior to labour so that the mother understands what medical procedures may be necessary for the safety of both she and her child.

Reasons for infertility include the trend toward delaying childbirth, the use of IUDs, and the rise in the incidence of pelvic inflammatory disease. Endometriosis is one of the leading causes of infertility in women, while low sperm count is the single largest fertility problem among men. There are a number of options available to couples with fertility problems. Overall success rates for fertility treatments range from 30 to 70 percent, depending on the specific cause of the infertility.

Learning Objectives

1. List permanent and reversible contraceptive methods, discuss their effectiveness in preventing pregnancy and the spread of sexually transmitted diseases, and describe how these methods are used.

2. Summarize the legal decisions surrounding abortion and the various types of abortion procedures used today.

3. Discuss emotional health, maternal health, financial evaluation, and contingency planning in terms of your own life's goals as aspects to consider before becoming parents.

4. Explain the importance of prenatal care and the process of pregnancy.

5. Describe the basic stages of childbirth as well as some of the complications that can arise during labour and delivery.

6. Review some of the primary causes of and possible solutions for infertility.

Key Terms

Fill in a brief definition to help you remember these terms.

fertility_____

conception _____

contraception_____

condom _____

contraceptive effectiveness rate_____

oral contraceptives_____

morning-after pill _____

diethylstilbestrol (DES)_____

spermicides _____

female condom _____

diaphragm _____

toxic shock syndrome (TSS) _____

cervical cap _____

intrauterine device (IUD) _____

withdrawal_____

Depo-Provera _____

Norplant _____

fertility awareness methods (FAM)_____

cervical mucus method _____

body temperature method _____

calendar method _____

sterilization _____

tubal ligation _____

hysterectomy _____

vasectomy _____

abortion _____

vacuum aspiration _____

dilation and evacuation (D&E) _____

dilation and curettage (D&C) _____

hysterectomy _____

induction abortion _____

preconception care _____

teratogenic_____

fetal alcohol syndrome (FAS) _____

Down's syndrome _____

human chorionic gonadotropin (HCG) _____

trimester _____

embryo _____

fetus_____

placenta _____

amniocentesis _____

amniotic sac _____

transition _____

episiotomy _____

perineum _____

afterbirth _____

postpartum depression _____

caesarean section (C-section) _____

miscarriage _____

Rh factor _____

ectopic pregnancy _____

stillbirth _____

infertility _____

pelvic inflammatory disease (PID) _____

endometriosis _____

low sperm count _____

fertility drugs _____

alternative insemination _____

in vitro fertilization _____

gamete intrafallopian transfer (GIFT) _____

nonsurgical embryo transfer _____

embryo transfer _____

embryo freezing _____

Critical Thinking Exercises

1. A woman wants to use the calendar method of fertility control. She keeps a record of her menstrual cycle for 12 months. Her shortest cycle is 26 days, Her longest cycle is 33 days. What are fertile days in her cycle? What days should she abstain from penis-vagina contact in order to avoid pregnancy?

2. Suppose you or your spouse just found out that you are expecting a child in eight months. Identify concerns for prenatal care that you would have.

3. Jenny just found out that she is six weeks pregnant. This is her first pregnancy and she does not know what to expect. Describe the changes that will occur during each trimester of her pregnancy.

4. Aiko is expecting a baby in two months. She is considering breast-feeding her baby. What are the advantages to breast-feeding? When deciding whether to breast- or bottle-feed, what should she consider?

5. Rashida is expecting her second child in 6 months. For her first child, she experienced a traditional hospital birth and was dissatisfied. What are her options for her second infant's birth and her participation in it?

Critical Thinking Activity: The Possibility of Parenthood

If you are sexually active, there is a chance that you or your partner could become pregnant. Choosing if and when to have children is a great responsibility. A woman and her partner have much to consider before planning or risking a pregnancy. Before you plan or risk a pregnancy, you have the responsibility to make certain you are physically, emotionally, and financially prepared to care for another human being. Assume you are about to become a parent and answer the following questions based upon this assumption.

1. Why do you want to have a child?
2. How will you financially provide for your child?
3. Will both you and your partner work or will one of you stay home with the child?
4. What health behaviours will you change for the sake of the unborn child?
5. What birth method will you choose? Why?
6. Who will you turn to for information on how to raise your child?
7. Will you need additional space in your home?
8. What parenting skills do you possess?
9. How much experience do you have raising children?
10. How will you provide for the child should something happen to you and your partner?

General Review Questions

Short Answer

1. What three conditions are necessary for conception?
2. What are the procedures for female and male sterilization?
3. What are some early signs of pregnancy?
4. Describe the stages in the birth process?
5. What are the risks associated with abortion?

Matching

1. Match the reversible methods of contraception with its definition.

   a. abstinence   g. cervical cap

   b. outercourse   h. oral contraceptives

   c. condom   i. progestin-only pills

   d. spermicides   j. morning-after pill

   e. female condom   k. intrauterine device

   f. diaphragm   l. withdrawal

   ___ 1. chemical substances that kill sperm

   ___ 2. a small cup made of latex that is designed to fit snugly over the entire cervix

   ___ 3. deliberately shunning intercourse

   ___ 4. pills taken daily for 3 weeks of the menstrual cycle to prevent ovulation through regulation of hormones

   ___ 5. a sheath of thin latex designed to fit over an erect penis and catch semen upon ejaculation

   ___ 6. oral-genital sex and mutual masturbation

   ___ 7. a soft, shallow cup made of thin latex rubber designed to fit snugly behind the pubic bone in front of the cervix and over the back of the cervix on the other side and used with spermicidal cream or jelly

   ___ 8. withdrawing the penis from the vagina before ejaculation

   ___ 9. single-use, loose-fitting polyurethane sheath designed as one unit with two diaphragm-like rings

   ___ 10. mini-pills that contain small doses of progesterone

   ___ 11. drugs taken within 3 days after intercourse to prevent fertilization or implantation

   ___ 12. a T-shaped plastic device that is implanted in the uterus to prevent conception

2. Match the following prenatal procedure with its purpose.

   a. fetoscopy

   b. amniocentesis

   c. ultrasound

   d. chorionic villi sampling

   ___ 1. This procedure reveals the presence of 40 genetic abnormalities, as well as the sex of the child.

   ___ 2. This procedure determines the size and position of the fetus and can also detect defects in the CNS and digestive system of the fetus.

   ___ 3. This procedure allows viewing the fetus directly.

   ___ 4. This procedure involves snipping tissue from the developing fetal sac for couples who are at high risk for having a baby with Down's syndrome or a debilitating hereditary disease.

Multiple Choice

1. Birth control pills, condoms, and abstinence are examples of:
   a. Permanent methods of contraception
   b. Reversible methods of contraception
   c. Temporary methods of contraception
   d. Transitional methods of contraception

2. Which of the following is(are) an early warning sign(s) for possible complications associated with oral contraceptive use?
   a. Abdominal pain
   b. Eye problems
   c. Headache
   d. All of the above

3. Women who smoke more than 10 to 15 cigarettes a day during pregnancy have higher rates of:
   a. Miscarriages
   b. Stillbirth
   c. Premature births
   d. All of the above

4. Modem pregnancy tests are designed to detect the presence of:
   a. HCG
   b. LH
   c. FSH
   d. RU-486

5. Toxic chemicals, pesticides, X-rays and other hazardous compounds that cause birth defects are referred to as:
   a. Carcinogens
   b. Teratogens
   c. Mutants
   d. Environmental assaults

6. Detection of major health defects in a fetus as early as the fourteenth to eighteenth weeks of pregnancy can be determined by what procedure?
   a. Ultrasound
   b. Fetoscopy
   c. Amniocentesis
   d. Sonography

7. During the second stage of labor:
   a. The amniotic sac breaks
   b. The baby shifts into a head down position
   c. The junction of the pubic bones loosens to permit expansion of the pelvic girth
   d. The uterus works to push the baby through the birth canal

8. The most popular birth alternative in the United States is:
   a. Leboyer method
   b. Harris method
   c. Lamaze method
   d. Eclectic method

9. Postpartum depression is characterized by:
   a. Energy depletion
   b. Anxiety
   c. Mood swings
   d. All of the above

10. During the third stage of labor:
    a. Contractions become more rhythmic and painful
    b. The amniotic sac breaks
    c. The baby shifts into a head-down position
    d. The placenta or afterbirth is expelled from the womb

11. Which of the following contraceptive method has the greatest failure rate?
    a. Chance
    b. Condoms
    c. Withdrawal
    d. Foams, suppositories, jellies, and creams

12. A soft, shallow cup made of thin latex rubber that is designed to cover the cervix and block access to the uterus is called:
    a. A condom
    b. A diaphragm
    c. An IUD
    d. A spermicidal sponge

13. The type of contraceptive that consists of six silicon capsules that are surgically inserted under the skin of a woman's upper arm is called:
    a. Depo-Provera
    b. Norplant
    c. Progesterone inserts
    d. Intradermal devices

14. The leading cause of infertility in women in the Canada is:
    a. Pelvic inflammatory disease
    b. Endometriosis
    c. Low sperm count
    d. Psychological stress

15. The fertilization of an egg in a test tube followed by transfer to a nutrient medium and subsequent transfer to the mother's body is called:
    a. Alternative insemination
    b. In vitro fertilization
    c. Gamete intrafallopian transfer
    d. Nonsurgical embryo transfer

16. A collection of symptoms, including mental retardation, slowed nerve reflexes and small head size, that can appear in infants of women who drink too much alcohol during pregnancy is called:
    a. Teratogenic poisoning
    b. Fetal Alcohol Syndrome
    c. Down's syndrome
    d. Tay-Sachs disease

17. The most common birth defect found in babies born to older mothers is:
    a. Hemophilia
    b. Anencephaly
    c. Down's syndrome
    d. Sickle cell anemia

18. Pregnancy usually lasts:
    a. 23 weeks
    b. 32 weeks
    c. 40 weeks
    d. 53 weeks

19. The surgical procedure in which the female's Fallopian tubes are closed or cut and cauterized to prevent access by sperm to released eggs is called:
    a. Tubal ligation
    b. Vasectomy
    c. Hysterectomy
    d. Abortion

20 Medical care that is received prior to becoming pregnant and helps a woman assess her potential maternal health is called:
    a. Precoital care
    b. Preconception care
    c. Prenatal care
    d. Genetic counseling

21. The estimated expense of raising a child from birth to 21 years of age, not including the cost of a college education, is:
    a. $75,000
    b. $150,000
    c. $200,000
    d. Over $250,000

22. Sudden Infant Death Syndrome is believed to occur when:
    a. A baby is exposed to high levels of folic acid
    b. A mother has undergone an extremely difficult delivery
    c. A mother experiences a traumatic shock during the prenatal development of the fetus
    d. An infant is under the age of one and suddenly dies for no apparent reason

23. An ectopic pregnancy occurs when:
    a. The fertilized egg implants outside the uterus
    b. There is a chromosomal birth defect present
    c. The mother is Rh positive and the fetus is Rh negative
    d. The fetus is not viable

24. While fetuses that are born during the seventh month may live, in order to survive:
    a. The fetus needs the layer of fat it acquires during the eighth month
    b. The fetus needs time for its organs to develop to their full potential
    c. The baby will usually require intensive medical care
    d. All of the above

25. Most oral contraceptives work through:
    a. The use of synthetic follicle-stimulating hormones
    b. The combined effects of synthetic estrogen and progesterone
    c. The combined effects of synthetic testosterone and follicle-stimulating hormones
    d. The use of estrogen-only hormones

26. Depo-Provera:
    a. Must be taken orally every 24 hours
    b. Consists of six silicone capsules that contain progesterone
    c. Is a long-acting synthetic progesterone that is injected intramuscularly every three months
    d. Must be inserted in the vagina at least 15 minutes prior to intercourse and left in place at least six hours afterwards

27. A released ovum can survive for up to ___hour(s) after ovulation, while sperm can live for as long as ___day(s) in the vagina.
    a. 24 hours; I day
    b. 30 hours; 2 days
    c. 43 hours; 3 days
    d. 48 hours; 5 days

28. A chemical substance that kills sperm is known as:
    a. Spermatogenesis
    b. Sperm barrier
    c. Spermicide
    d. All of the above

29. Sterilization of the male that consists of cutting and tying both vas deferens is called a:
    a. Vasectomy
    b. Tuba] ligation
    c. Circumcision
    d. None of the above

30. Low sperm count in males can result from:
    a. The mumps virus
    b. Excessively tight underwear or outerwear
    c. Varicose veins
    d. All of the above

Language Enrichment Glossary

In addition to the words in the Key Terms list at the end of the chapter, students listed the following words as difficult to understand. Use the chapter Key Terms list, this list, your dictionary, and teachers and friends to learn the meaning of words you do not understand.

adage:	saying
affords:	gives, allows
ascertain:	determine
at risk for:	in danger of
attributable to:	caused by
barrier:	a block
burrows:	buries or digs itself into
calculated:	figured
cervical:	related to the opening of the uterus
clots:	thickened lumps of blood
complications:	related problems
comprehensive:	broad, including many things
compromising:	risky
conducive:	favourable
constitute:	make up
contractions:	muscle squeezing
conventional:	customary, standard
debilitating:	weakening
depletion:	lowering
differentiates:	separates
discernible:	understandable, discoverable
disintegrate:	break apart, decay
dislodged:	moved out of place
emits:	sends out
ensure:	guarantee
entail:	involve, require
hemorrhage:	bleeding which doesn't stop
impose:	place, force
in conjunction with:	together with
inflammatory:	becoming red, swollen and painful
intramuscularly:	into the muscle
lesions:	open wounds
metabolizes:	how a substance acts in the body
misshapen:	shaped incorrectly
readily:	easily
render:	result in, cause to be
reversible:	able to change back to original
revert:	go back to, return
shunning:	avoiding
sluggish:	slow

spontaneous:	happening without planning
stump:	short end left after being cut
subsequent:	following
succumbing:	giving in
suffice:	be enough
suppresses:	stops
synthetic:	artificial, human-made
toxic:	poisonous, harmful
transfusion:	adding blood to the bloodstream
undue:	too much, excessive
viable:	living

CHAPTER 7
Nutrition: Eating for Optimum Health

Chapter Overview

Nutrition is the science that investigates the relationship between physiological functions and the essential elements of the foods we eat. Many people have difficulty finding the 'right balance between eating to maintain body functions and eating to satisfy our appetites. Developing the right nutritional plan is an essential health-promoting skill. Calories are eaten in the form of proteins, fats, and carbohydrates, three of the basic nutrients necessary for life. Vitamins, minerals, and water are also necessary nutrients but do not contain any calories. The relative proportion of nutrients in our diets and our lack of physical activity cause weight problems and resultant diseases. For instance, a high concentration of saturated fats in the Canadian diet increases our risk for heart disease. Canada's Food Guide illustrates the importance of grains, cereals, vegetables, and fruits compared to meat, fish, poultry, dairy products, and other foods. It is a useful guide to daily food choices.

Water is necessary for human survival and maintenance of bodily functions. It is the most abundant substance in the human body, making up between 50 and 60 percent of our total body weight. Proteins are the essential constituents of nearly all body cells. Proteins are necessary for the development and repair of bone, muscle, skin, and blood, and are the key elements of antibodies, enzymes, and hormones. Carbohydrates are the major energy suppliers of the body. There are two major types of carbohydrates: simple sugars and complex carbohydrates. Fibre helps move foods through the digestive system and softens stools by absorbing large quantities of water. Fats are necessary for the maintenance of healthy skin and hair, insulation of body organs against shock, maintenance of body temperature, and the proper functioning of cells; however, fats must be consumed in moderation. Vitamins promote growth and help maintain life and health. Vitamins are either water soluble or fat soluble. Minerals aid physiological processes within the body. Without minerals, vitamins could not be absorbed. Although minerals are necessary for body function, there are limits to the amount we should consume. We tend to overuse or underuse certain minerals. Because men and women differ in body size, body composition, and overall metabolic rates, they have different nutritional needs throughout the life cycle.

Between 3 and 7 percent of Canadians today claim to be some form of vegetarian. If vegetarians combine the right types of food, they ensure proper nutrient intake. A food guide pyramid that conveys all the essentials of a vegetarian diet was devised in 1994.

University and college students often face a challenge when trying to eat healthy foods. But there are many tips for making healthy food choices. For instance, fast foods are not necessarily unhealthy. It is possible to eat healthy food by taking some simple steps, such as asking for nutritional analyses of items and ordering foods without the extras. To ensure a quality diet when funds are short, take steps such as using coupons, shopping at discount warehouse food chains, planning ahead to get the most for your dollar, and cooking large meals and freezing smaller portions for later use.

Food irradiation, food-borne illness, food allergies, and other food-safety concerns are becoming increasingly important to well-informed consumers. Learning potential risks and taking preventive measures are part of a good nutritional plan.

Learning Objectives

1. Examine the factors that influence dietary decisions and discuss how the Canada Food Guide can be used to help break bad habits.

2. Explain major essential nutrients (water, proteins, carbohydrates, fibre, fats, vitamins, and minerals) and indicate what purpose they serve in maintaining your overall health.

3. Define the different types of vegetarianism and discuss possible health benefits and risks.

4. Describe the unique problems that students may have when trying to eat healthy foods and the actions they can take to insure compliance with the food guide.

5. Explain some of the food safety concerns of which consumers should be aware, including food irradiation, food-borne illnesses, food allergies, and other food health concerns.

Key Terms

Fill in a brief definition to help you remember these terms.

hunger _____

appetite _____

nutrition _____

nutrients _____

calorie _____

digestive process _____

saliva _____

esophagus _____

stomach _____

small intestine _____

dehydration _____

proteins _____

amino acids _____

essential amino acids _____

complete (high-quality) proteins _____

incomplete proteins _____

carbohydrates _____

simple sugars _____

complex carbohydrates _____

monosaccharide _____

disaccharide _____

polysaccharide _____

cellulose _____

glycogen _____

fats _____

triglyceride _____

cholesterol _____

plaque _____

high-density lipoproteins (HDLs) _____

low-density !ipoproteins (LDLs) _____

saturated fats _____

unsaturated fats _____

trans-fatty acids _____

vitamins _____

hypervitaminosis _____

minerals _____

macrominerals _____

trace minerals _____

anemia _____

vegetarian _____

food irradiation _____

food allergies_____

cross reactivity _____

food intolerance_____

organically grown _____

Critical Thinking Exercises

1. After reading this chapter, you no doubt have been able to decipher solid nutritional information from myths, untruths, and half-truths about a good nutritional plan. What are some of the myths you have held about nutrition? What information have you learned in this chapter that debunks these myths?

2. Suppose you are a nutritionist for a residence hall and have been asked to explain to the cafeteria staff how to ensure that students receive the essential nutrients. Explain to the staff how students can obtain the necessary water, proteins, carbohydrates, fibre, fats, vitamins, and minerals.

3. Suppose you are a nutritionist in a hospital. A patient who is ready to be discharged needs to reduce his fat intake. What guidelines will help him to reduce his fat intake?

4. John is a truck driver and eats a lot while on the road. He is concerned about how healthy his food choices are at fast food restaurants. What suggestions do you have that will ensure John's healthy eating?

5. A social worker is helping a single mother and her three children maintain nutritional eating, despite a lack of funds. What steps can this family take to ensure a quality diet?

6. As manager of student residential apartment housing, you are concerned about preventing food-borne illnesses. Construct a handout to be distributed to all residents on how to prevent food-borne illnesses.

Critical Thinking Activity: A Menu of Food Choices

Canada's Food Guide illustrates the importance of grains, cereals, vegetables, and fruits compared to meat, fish, poultry, dairy products, and other foods. It serves as a guide to daily food choices. In order to better understand the importance of good nutrition, develop your own menu of food choices for one week using the Food Guide and the following menu outline.

Menu

Sunday

Breakfast

    Bread, Cereal, Rice, and Pasta Group-

    Vegetable Group-

    Fruit Group-

    Milk, Yogurt, and Cheese Group-

    Meat, Poultry, Fish, Dry Beans, Eggs, and Nuts Group-

    Fats, Oils, and Sweets-

Lunch

    Bread, Cereal, Rice, and Pasta Group-

    Vegetable Group-

    Fruit Group-

    Milk, Yogurt, and Cheese Group-

    Meat, Poultry, Fish, Dry Beans, Eggs, and Nuts Group-

    Fats, Oils, and Sweets-

Dinner

    Bread, Cereal, Rice, and Pasta Group-

    Vegetable Group-

    Fruit Group-

    Milk, Yogurt, and Cheese Group-

    Meat, Poultry, Fish, Dry Beans, Eggs, and Nuts Group-

    Fats, Oils, and Sweets-

Monday

Breakfast

Bread, Cereal, Rice, and Pasta Group-

Vegetable Group-

Fruit Group-

Milk, Yogurt, and Cheese Group-

Meat, Poultry, Fish, Dry Beans, Eggs, and Nuts Group-

Fats, Oils, and Sweets-

Lunch

Bread, Cereal, Rice, and Pasta Group-

Vegetable Group-

Fruit Group-

Milk, Yogurt, and Cheese Group-

Meat, Poultry, Fish, Dry Beans, Eggs, and Nuts Group-

Fats, Oils, and Sweets-

Dinner

Bread, Cereal, Rice, and Pasta Group-

Vegetable Group-

Fruit Group-

Milk, Yogurt, and Cheese Group-

Meat, Poultry, Fish, Dry Beans, Eggs, and Nuts Group-

Fats, Oils, and Sweets-

Tuesday

Breakfast

Bread, Cereal, Rice, and Pasta Group-

Vegetable Group-

Fruit Group-

Milk, Yogurt, and Cheese Group-

Meat, Poultry, Fish, Dry Beans, Eggs, and Nuts Group-

Fats, Oils, and Sweets-

Lunch

Bread, Cereal, Rice, and Pasta Group-

Vegetable Group-

Fruit Group-

Milk, Yogurt, and Cheese Group-

Meat, Poultry, Fish, Dry Beans, Eggs, and Nuts Group-

Fats, Oils, and Sweets-

Dinner

Bread, Cereal, Rice, and Pasta Group-

Vegetable Group-

Fruit Group-

Milk, Yogurt, and Cheese Group-

Meat, Poultry, Fish, Dry Beans, Eggs, and Nuts Group-

Fats, Oils, and Sweets-

Wednesday

Breakfast

Bread, Cereal, Rice, and Pasta Group-

Vegetable Group-

Fruit Group-

Milk, Yogurt, and Cheese Group-

Meat, Poultry, Fish, Dry Beans, Eggs, and Nuts Group-

Fats, Oils, and Sweets-

Lunch

Bread, Cereal, Rice, and Pasta Group-

Vegetable Group-

Fruit Group-

Milk, Yogurt, and Cheese Group-

Meat, Poultry, Fish, Dry Beans, Eggs, and Nuts Group-

Fats, Oils, and Sweets-

Dinner

Bread, Cereal, Rice, and Pasta Group-

Vegetable Group-

Fruit Group-

Milk, Yogurt, and Cheese Group-

Meat, Poultry, Fish, Dry Beans, Eggs, and Nuts Group-

Fats, Oils, and Sweets-

Thursday

Breakfast

Bread, Cereal, Rice, and Pasta Group-

Vegetable Group-

Fruit Group-

Milk, Yogurt, and Cheese Group-

Meat, Poultry, Fish, Dry Beans, Eggs, and Nuts Group-

Fats, Oils, and Sweets-

Lunch

Bread, Cereal, Rice, and Pasta Group-

Vegetable Group-

Fruit Group-

Milk, Yogurt, and Cheese Group-

Meat, Poultry, Fish, Dry Beans, Eggs, and Nuts Group-

Fats, Oils, and Sweets-

Dinner

Bread, Cereal, Rice, and Pasta Group-

Vegetable Group-

Fruit Group-

Milk, Yogurt, and Cheese Group-

Meat, Poultry, Fish, Dry Beans, Eggs, and Nuts Group-

Fats, Oils, and Sweets-

Friday

Breakfast

    Bread, Cereal, Rice, and Pasta Group-

    Vegetable Group-

    Fruit Group-

    Milk, Yogurt, and Cheese Group-

    Meat, Poultry, Fish, Dry Beans, Eggs, and Nuts Group-

    Fats, Oils, and Sweets-

Lunch

    Bread, Cereal, Rice, and Pasta Group-

    Vegetable Group-

    Fruit Group-

    Milk, Yogurt, and Cheese Group-

    Meat, Poultry, Fish, Dry Beans, Eggs, and Nuts Group-

    Fats, Oils, and Sweets-

Dinner

    Bread, Cereal, Rice, and Pasta Group-

    Vegetable Group-

    Fruit Group-

    Milk, Yogurt, and Cheese Group-

    Meat, Poultry, Fish, Dry Beans, Eggs, and Nuts Group-

    Fats, Oils, and Sweets-

Saturday

Breakfast

Bread, Cereal, Rice, and Pasta Group-

Vegetable Group-

Fruit Group-

Milk, Yogurt, and Cheese Group-

Meat, Poultry, Fish, Dry Beans, Eggs, and Nuts Group-

Fats, Oils, and Sweets-

Lunch

Bread, Cereal, Rice, and Pasta Group-

Vegetable Group-

Fruit Group-

Milk, Yogurt, and Cheese Group-

Meat, Poultry, Fish, Dry Beans, Eggs, and Nuts Group-

Fats, Oils, and Sweets-

Dinner

Bread, Cereal, Rice, and Pasta Group-

Vegetable Group-

Fruit Group-

Milk, Yogurt, and Cheese Group-

Meat, Poultry, Fish, Dry Beans, Eggs, and Nuts Group

Fats, Oils, and Sweets-

Questions for the Critical Thinker

After you have completed your menu, reflect on the following questions. Your thoughtful responses will enhance your learning of this **Critical Thinking Activity** as well as your understanding of nutrition.

1. What did you learn about your nutritional choices from preparing a menu?
2. Was it easy or difficult to get all the recommended servings in each food group?
3. What changes do you need to make in your diet to ensure that you meet the pyramid requirements?
4. What modifications in food preparation can you make to use fats, oils, and sweets sparingly?

General Review Questions

Short Answer

1. Define a calorie.
2. Explain how the digestive process works.
3. What are the two major types of carbohydrates?
4. What are the benefits of fibre?
5. Distinguish between high-density lipoproteins and low-density lipoproteins?
6. Distinguish between saturated and unsaturated fats.

Multiple Choice

1 . The science that investigates the relationship between physiological function and the essential elements of foods we eat is:
a. Nutrition
b. Dietology
c. Metabolic studies
d. Home economics

2. The feeling associated with physiological need to eat is called:
a. Appetite
b. Nutrition
c. Hunger
d. Nutritional survival

3. The nutrient that aids in fluid and electrolyte balance, maintains pH balance, and transports molecules and cells throughout the body is:
a. Water
b. Minerals
c. Vitamins
d. Fat

4. Substances that are made up of amino acids that are major components of cells are:
a. Water
b. Carbohydrates
c. Proteins
d. Minerals

5. Complete proteins are obtained from:
a. Red meats
b. Poultry
c. Fish
d. All of the above

6. The type of carbohydrates that are primarily found in grains, cereals, dark green leafy vegetables and cruciferous vegetables is:
a. Simple carbohydrates
b. Complex carbohydrates
c. Glucose
d. Dextrose

7. The nutrient that supplies us with the energy needed to sustain normal daily activity is:
   a. Protein
   b. Vitamins
   c. Carbohydrates
   d. Fiber

8. The best way to increase dietary fiber is to:
   a. Eat more meat
   b. Eat more complex carbohydrates
   c. Decrease the amount of water to 3-4 glasses per day
   d. Decrease the amount of fruit while increasing beans and nuts

9. Fiber found to be a factor in lowering blood cholesterol and thereby reducing the risk of cardiovascular disease is called:
   a. Alpha cellulose
   b. Triglycerides
   c. Soluble fiber
   d. Insoluble fiber

10. Compounds that facilitate the transportation of cholesterol in the blood to the liver for metabolism and elimination from the body are:
    a. Plaque
    b. High-density lipoproteins
    c. Low-density lipoproteins
    d. Very low-density lipoproteins

11. When too many calories are consumed:
    a. The excess is excreted from the body
    b. The body works harder to " burn" the calories
    c. The excess is converted in the liver into triglycerides, and stored throughout our bodies
    d. The excess is circulated until it is burned as energy

12. Calcium is vital to the body because:
    a. It builds strong bones and teeth
    b. It regulates heartbeat
    c. It is vital to nerve impulse transmission
    d. All of the above

13. The mineral folate has been shown to:
    a. Reduce the risk for colon cancer

b. Decrease spina bifida and other neural tube defects in infants
c. Decrease hypertension and diabetes
d. Increase the risk for breast cancer

14. To prevent the chance of food-borne illness at home, a person should:
    a. Wash their hands with soap and water before working with food or eating
    b. Eat leftovers within three days
    c. When shopping, put meats in separate plastic bags to prevent meat juices from dripping onto other foods
    d. All of the above

15. While eating, Jenny begins to have difficulty breathing and her face begins to swell. This may indicate that:
    a. She is having food that is very spicy and may need to avoid foods with chili peppers
    b. She may be experiencing an anaphylactic reaction to her food and may require a shot of epinephrine
    c. She may have a food-borne illness
    d. All of the above

16. Fats that generally come from animals are called:
    a. Polyunsaturated fats
    b. Monounsaturated fats
    c. Saturated fats
    d. Low density lipoproteins

17. The recommended number of servings each day from the bread, cereals, rice, and pasta group is:
    a. 2-4 servings
    b. 3-5 servings
    c. 4-5 servings
    d. 6-11 servings

18. The process by which foods are broken down and either absorbed or excreted by the body is known as the:
    a. Digestive process
    b. Elimination process
    c. Metabolism process
    d. Nutritional process

19. A major factor in the tendency to be overweight is:
    a. A diet containing 48% of the total calories from complex carbohydrates
    b. Insufficient dietary intake of Vitamin A & C
    c. Excess calorie consumption
    d. A diet containing less than 30% of the calories from protein

20. If the body does not have sufficient water and becomes depleted of fluids:
    a. Serious problems can result within a matter of hours and after a few days death is likely
    b. Malnutrition will result due to lack of sufficient vitamins
    c. The body's defense system will increase antibody production
    d. The body will release hormones to increase metabolism

21. Amino acids that must be obtained from food are referred to as:
    a. Nonessential amino acids
    b. Essential amino acids
    c. Complete amino acids
    d. Incomplete amino acids

22. The type of simple sugar that is found in corn syrup, honey, molasses, vegetables, and fruit is:
    a. Simple carbohydrates
    b. Complex carbohydrates
    c. Glucose
    d. Dextrose

23. Oat bran and dried beans, especially kidney beans) are major sources of:
    a. Alpha cellulose
    b. Triglycerides
    c. Soluble fiber
    d. Insoluble fiber

24. The most common form of fat circulating in the blood is:
    a. Cholesterol
    b. Triglyceride
    c. Saturated fat
    d. Unsaturated fat

25. The nutrient that is vital for the maintenance of healthy skin and hair, insulates the body organs against shock and maintains body temperature is:
    a. Carbohydrates
    b. Water
    c. Protein
    d. Fat

26. A major cause of atherosclerosis is:
    a. Plaque
    b. High density lipoproteins
    c. Unsaturated fats
    d. Monounsaturated fats

27. Fatty acids that have unusual shapes and are produced when polyunsaturated oils are hydrogenated are called:
    a. Saturated fats
    b. Unsaturated fats
    c. Cholesterol
    d. Trans-fatty acids

28. Which of the following is not a fat-soluble vitamin?
    a. Vitamin A
    b. Vitamin B
    c. Vitamin D
    d. Vitamin K

29. Inorganic, indestructible elements that aid physiological processes within the body are:
    a. Vitamins
    b. Amino acids
    c. Minerals
    d. High density lipoproteins

30. For every three servings of fruits or vegetables per day, men can expect:
    a. Improved regulation of blood and body fluids
    b. A 50% reduction the risk of colon cancer
    c. A 14% reduction in pancreatic cancer
    d. A 22% lower risk of stroke

Language Enrichment Glossary

In addition to the words in the Key Terms list at the end of the chapter, students listed the following words as difficult to understand. Use the chapter Key Terms list, this list, your dictionary, and teachers and friends to learn the meaning of words you do not understand.

adverse: negative
bombard: heavy attack
bulges: swellings
clarifies: makes clear
constipation: unable to make bowel movement
constraints: limits
convert: change
culprit: source of trouble, guilty person
dire: threatening, serious
discriminating: choosing carefully
duped: fooled, tricked
entice: tempt
essential: necessary
formidable: overwhelming
landmark: important stage of development
lobbied: attempted to persuade
maligned: criticized
mounting: increasing
optimum: maximum
pesticides: chemicals used to kill insects
potent: strong
pouches: small pockets
preliminary: introductory
residual: remaining, left over
resounding: strong
sift: sort
skim milk: milk with most of the fat removed
skimp: economize, cut back on
soluble: easily dissolved in liquid
soy milk: drink made from soybean liquid
stem: come from

CHAPTER 8
Managing Your Weight: Finding a Healthy Balance

Chapter Overview

You need to gather accurate information about weight loss products and services, to learn what triggers your "eat" buttons, and to analyze your lifestyle to determine your problem areas. Managing your weight also involves developing skills to set rational weight loss goals and using social and community supports. Whether you are overweight is somewhat subjective and depends on your body structure and how your weight is distributed. Traditionally, people have compared their weight with data from some form of standard height-and-weight chart, which gives the "ideal" weight for males and females of given height and frame size. One of the most reliable height-weight guides is the Metropolitan Life Height and Weight Table. Recently, obesity has been redefined. Although body weight is certainly an important factor, the real measure of obesity is how much fat your body contains. Obesity is generally defined as an accumulation of fat beyond what is considered normal for a person's age, sex, and body type. There are a variety of methods available for assessing body fat, including hydrostatic weighing techniques, the pinch test, the skinfold caliper test, girth and circumference measures, body mass index, soft-tissue roentgenogram, bioelectric impedance analysis, and total body electrical conductivity.

There are many possible causes of obesity, including: heredity, hunger, appetite, and satiety; excessive number of fat cells; setpoint theory; endocrine influence; psychosocial factors; eating cues; lack of awareness; metabolic changes; life-style; individuality; and the role of gender in obesity.

The two ways to lose weight are to decrease caloric intake and to increase exercise. Increasing your basal metabolic rate, your resting metabolic rate, or your exercise metabolic rate will help burn calories. Most health authorities recommend that, rather than going on a diet, a person should adopt nutritional dietary changes and a program of increased activity aimed at changing metabolic rates and increasing muscle strength. Improving the way you eat involves breaking old habits. First, determine what triggers your eating behaviour. Usually, these dietary "triggers" centre on problems in everyday living rather than real hunger pangs. Keeping a detailed diary of the triggers will help you understand what causes you to want food. Once you recognize the factors, removing the triggers or substituting other activities for them will help you develop more healthy eating patterns. Successful weight control includes setting realistic goals, such as trying to lose a healthy I to 2 pounds a week; seeking help from reputable sources in selecting a dietary plan; and avoiding fasting, starvation diets, and very low calorie diets. Some people are chronically underweight for metabolic, hereditary, or other reasons. Strategies for putting on needed pounds include reducing exercise, eating more high calorie foods, and learning to relax.

Persons suffering from eating disorders have such an extreme tear of being fat that they engage in behaviours such as self-starvation, bingeing, vomiting, excessive exercise, and/or purging. Anorexia nervosa is characterized by excessive preoccupation with food, self-starvation, and/or extreme exercising to achieve weight loss. Bulimia nervosa is characterized by binge eating followed by inappropriate compensating measures taken to prevent weight gain. Binge eating refers to recurrent binge eating without excessive measures to lose the weight gained during binges. The most effective treatment for eating disorders combines different approaches into a package that involves the patient and his or her family and friends.

Learning Objectives

1. Describe how healthy weight is determined both by weight and in terms of body content; describe the major techniques for body content assessment.

2. Describe those factors that place people at risk for problems with obesity.

3. Discuss the roles of exercise, dieting, nutrition, "miracle diets," and other strategies in weight control.

4. Describe the three major eating disorders and explain the health risks of these conditions.

Key Terms

Fill in a brief definition to help you remember these terms.

obesity _____

hydrostatic weighing techniques _____

pinch test _____

skinfold caliper test _____

girth and circumference measures_____

body mass index (BMI)_____

soft-tissue roentgenogram _____

bioelectrical impedance analysis (BIA) _____

total body electrical conductivity (TOBEC) _____

adaptive thermogenesis _____

brown fat cells_____

hunger _____

appetite _____

satiety _____

hyperplasia _____

hypertrophy _____

setpoint theory_____

plateau _____

thyroid gland _____

basal metabolic rate (BMR) _____

yo-yo diet_____

resting metabolic rate (RMR) _____

exercise metabolic rate (EMR) _____

very low calorie diets (VLCDs) _____

ketosis _____

eating disorder_____

anorexia nervosa _____

bulimia nervosa_____

binge eating disorder (BED) _____

Critical Thinking Exercises

1. Kira is a 22-year-old student. She goes to the health centre for a weight assessment. She tells the technician that she is 5' 6" (168 cm) and 135 pounds (61.5 Kg.). What is Kira's body mass index? Is she in a desirable range?

2. At 140 pounds (64 Kg.) , Rhonda went on a diet to lose 25 pounds (11.5 Kg.). When she dropped to 130 pounds (59 Kg.) , she still wanted to lose 15 pounds (6.8 Kg.) to meet her goal. But she found that she had difficulty losing any additional weight. How does the setpoint theory explain Rhonda's difficulty in losing weight?

3. Forty-year-old Brenda decides that she needs to change her eating habits. What steps can she take to determine what triggers her eating? How can she remove the triggers or substitute other activities for them to help her develop more sensible eating patterns?

4. When Steve was home from college for his spring break vacation, he overheard his younger sister vomiting in the bathroom. When he asked her if she was sick, she denied that it had happened. He also noticed that she had lost a lot of weight and didn't eat at family meals. She constantly weighs herself and says she is "too fat." Steve believes that she has anorexia nervosa and needs serious medical help. What role can Steve take in getting her help?

Critical Thinking Activity: How Healthy Are Your Eating Habits?

Assessing your eating attitudes and behaviours will help identify if you are in danger of developing anorexia nervosa or bulimia nervosa. The majority of persons suffering from an eating disorder are female. Answer the following questions carefully.

- Do I refuse to maintain my body weight over a minimal normal weight for my age and height?
- Am I afraid of gaining weight or becoming fat, even though I have been told that I am underweight?
- Do I often "feel fat"?
- Do I have amenorrhea?
- Do I engage in recurrent episodes of binge eating (eating a large amount of food in a discrete period of time)?
- Do I regularly engage in self-induced vomiting in order to prevent weight gain?
- Do I regularly use laxatives or diuretics in order to prevent weight gain?
- Do I engage in vigorous exercise in order to prevent weight gain?
- Do I have at least two binge eating episodes a week for the duration of at least three months?
* Am I consistently over-concerned about my body shape and weight?

If you answered yes to one or more of these questions, you may be at risk for developing an eating disorder. Consult with a counsellor, an eating disorder clinic, a local hospital, or your student health centre for more information.

General Review Questions

Short Answer

1. Distinguish between essential fat and storage fat.
2. What three body types were identified by Harvard psychologist William Sheldon?
3. Distinguish between hunger and appetite.
4. What factors influence the basal metabolic rate?
5. What strategies can be used to change your eating habits and to select a nutritional plan that is right for you?
6. Identify symptoms of anorexia nervosa and bulimia nervosa.

Multiple Choice

1. In general, a person is classified "obese" when they are:
   a. 5%-10% above their ideal weight
   b. 10%-20% above their ideal weight
   c. 20%-30% above their ideal weight
   d. 40%-50% above their ideal weight

2. An accumulation of fat beyond what is considered normal for a person's age, sex, and body type is called:
   a. Body composition
   b. Obesity
   c. Overweight
   d. Body fat

3. The ratio of lean body mass to fat body mass is:
   a. Obesity
   b. Body composition
   c. Overweight mass ratio
   d. Obesity ratio

4. The technique of body fat assessment that utilizes electrical currents that are passed through fat and lean tissue is called:
   a. Body Mass Index
   b. Hydrostatic weight technique
   c. Bioelectrical impedance analysis
   d. Soft-tissue roentgenogram

5. The ideal total body fat for women is:
   a. 11-15%
   b. 18-22%
   c. 23-29%
   d. 27-35%

6. Essential fat makes up approximately percent of total body weight in men and approximately ___ percent of total body weight in women.
   a. 3 to 5; 18
   b. 3 to 7; 15
   c. 5 to 25; 13
   d. 3 to 5; 7

7. The part of the brain that regulates appetite and closely monitors levels of certain nutrients in the blood is the:
   a. Pituitary gland
   b. Hypothalamus
   c. Cerebral cortex
   d. Cerebellum

8. The theory of weight loss that proposes that a person's body has a set amount of weight at which it is programmed to be comfortable is called:
   a. Thermostatic maintenance theory
   b. Setpoint theory
   c. Plateau theory
   d. Endocrine balance theory

9. Most authorities argue that only ___ percent of the obese population have a thyroid problem that is attributed to obesity.
   a. 3-5
   b. 10-17
   c. 23-27
   d. 35-37

10. What percentage of all the calories you consume on a given day go to support your basal metabolism (i.e. heartbeat, breathing, maintaining body temperature, etc.)?
    a. 20-30%
    b. 40-60%
    c. 60-70%
    d. 75-85%

11. One pound of body fat contains approximately:
    a. 35 kilocalories
    b. 350 kilocalories
    c. 3,500 kilocalories
    d. 5,000 kilocalories

12. An acute form of self-starvation motivated by a fear of gaining weight and a severe disturbance in the perception of one's body is called:
    a. Anorexia nervosa
    b. Bulimia
    c. Binge/purge syndrome
    d. Compulsive eating disorder

13. A condition in which the body adapts to prolonged fasting or carbohydrate deprivation by converting body fat to ketones, which can be used as fuel for some brain activity is called:
    a. Caloric adaptation
    b. Carbohydrate synthesis
    c. Acidosis
    d. Ketones

14. Fat that is necessary for normal physiological functioning is called:
    a. Body fat
    b. Essential fat
    c. Brown fat
    d. Storage fat

15. An inborn physiological response to nutritional needs is:
    a. Hunger
    b. Appetite
    c. Satiety
    d. Adaptive thermogenesis

16. The ideal total body fat for men is:
    a. 5-10%
    b. 11-15%
    c. 16-20%
    d. 25-35%

17. The method of determining body fat by measuring the amount of water displaced when a person is completely submerged is called:
    a. Skin-fold caliper test
    b. Body mass index
    c. Hydrostatic weighing technique
    d. Bioelectrical impedance analysis

18. A medical standard used to define obesity using an index of the relationship of height and weight is the:
    a. Body composition index
    b. Body mass index
    c. Hydrostatic weight
    d. Waist-to-hip ratio

19. The mechanism in which the brain regulates metabolic activity according to caloric intake is called:
    a. Adaptive thermogenesis
    b. Hunger
    c. Satiety
    d. Appetite

20 Appetite is:
    a. Controlled by specialized fat cells known as brown cells
    b. An inborn physiological response to nutritional needs
    c. A learned response to food that is tied to an emotional or psychological craving for food that is often unrelated to nutritional needs
    d. None of the above

21. The gland, located in the throat, that produces a hormone that regulates metabolism is the:
    a. Lymph gland
    b. Thyroid gland
    c. Adrenal gland
    d. Pancreas

22. Eating food from fast-food restaurants is a problem because:
    a. Fast food is high in calories
    b. Fast food is eaten quickly so that there is not enough time for the "I'm full" signal
    c. Proportions tend to be bigger than they should be and tend to get eaten
    d. All of the above

23. The desire to "look good" that has a destructive and sometimes disabling affect on one's ability to function effectively in relationships and interactions with others is called:
    a. Appearance anxiety
    b. Obesity anxiety
    c. Social physique anxiety
    d. Anorexia nervosa

24. The best way to lose weight is:
    a. To lower calories
    b. To increase exercise
    c. To stagger calorie intake low or high calories on alternating days
    d. Both a and b

25. Approximately 90 percent of the daily calorie expenditures of most people occur as a result of:
    a. Basal metabolic rate
    b. Resting metabolic rate
    c. Exercise metabolic rate
    d. Sedentary metabolic rate

26. The major cause of low activity levels is:
    a. Vacuum cleaners
    b. Automobiles
    c. TV remote controls
    d. All of the above

27. The best way to improve one's chance for longterm success with weight loss is:
    a. Plan for nutrient-dense foods
    b. Plan for plateaus
    c. Chart your progress
    d. All of the above

28. An eating disorder among clinically obese individuals who binge eat much more often than the typical obese person is called:
    a. Anorexia nervosa
    b. Bulimia nervosa
    c. Binge/purge syndrome
    d. Binge eating disorder

29. Diets with caloric intake of 400 to 700 calories are called:
    a. Cambridge diet
    b. Liquid diets
    c. Jenny Craig
    d. Very low calorie diets

30. A man would be considered obese if his body fat exceeds ____ percent of his total body mass while a woman is considered obese if her body fat is ____percent of her total body mass.
    a. 15; 20
    b. 20; 30
    c. 35; 45
    d. 40; 50

Language Enrichment Glossary

In addition to the words in the Key Terms list at the end of the chapter, students listed the following words as difficult to understand. Use the chapter Key Terms list, this list, your dictionary, and teachers and friends to learn the meaning of words you do not understand.

abound:	overflow
appreciably:	significantly
bingeing:	uncontrolled eating
bolstered:	encouraged
bombard:	assault, overwhelm
buff:	very muscular
chronically:	persistently, repeatedly
composed:	made up of

comprehensive:	complete, thorough
controversial:	contradictory, debatable
corset:	tight undergarment to shape breasts, waist and hips
credentials:	qualifications
deplete:	to consume
diminish:	reduce
elect:	choose
equated:	associated
errant:	abnormal
essence:	basically
exemplify:	represent
gluttony:	excessive appetite
host:	large number
mechanics:	processes
morbidly:	extremely unhealthful
organic:	physical
phenomenon:	occurrence, happening
plateau:	level point
plausibility:	believability
predominance:	common occurrence
premises:	guidelines
proponents:	supporters
qualitative:	regarding quality
quantitative:	regarding quantity
quest:	search
rational:	realistic
reappraisal:	reassessment
recoil:	to pull back in fear
reputable:	good reputation
sabotage:	undermine, disable
satiety:	fullness
sedentary:	inactive
sloth:	inactivity, laziness
sophisticated:	refined, complex

CHAPTER 9
Personal Fitness: Improving Your Health Through Exercise

Chapter Overview

Regular physical activity improves more than 50 various physiological, metabolic, and psychological aspects of human life. Physiological rewards of exercise include improved cardiorespiratory efficiency, skeletal mass, weight control, health and life span. Psychological rewards of exercise include increased ability to cope with stress and improved self-esteem. Physical fitness is measured by cardiorespiratory endurance, flexibility, muscular strength, and muscular endurance.

The main category of physical activity known to enhance cardiovascular fitness is aerobic exercise. You will need to adjust the frequency, intensity, and duration of your aerobic activity program to accommodate your level of cardiovascular fitness. The recommended frequency of physical activity is three to five times per week. Monitoring exercise intensity is important. A target heart rate of 70 percent of maximum is known as the "conversational level of exercise" because you are able to talk with a partner while exercising. If you can sustain a conversational level of aerobic exercise for 20 to 30 minutes, you will improve your cardiovascular fitness.

Flexibility is a measure of the range of motion, or the amount of movement possible, at a particular joint. Flexibility is enhanced by static and dynamic stretching.

Muscular strength and endurance are maximized by following three key principles: the tension principle, the overload principle, and the specificity of training principle. Your skeletal muscles act in three different modes —isometric, concentric, and eccentric. There are four commonly used methods of applying resistance to develop strength and endurance:body weight, fixed, variable, and accommodating resistance.

The most frequent cause of injury associated with fitness activities is overtraining. There are two basic types of injuries caused by participation in fitness-related activities:overuse and traumatic. For personal fitness activities, appropriate exercise clothing and equipment are essential. Three of the most frequent injuries from repetitive overuse during exercise are plantar fasciitis, "shin splints," and "runner's knee." First-aid treatment for virtually all personal fitness injuries involves rest, ice, compression, and elevation. Exercising in extreme temperatures heightens your risk for a heat-related injury. The three different heat stress illnesses are progressive in their level of severity:heat cramps, heat exhaustion, and heat stroke. When you exercise in cool to cold weather, especially in windy conditions, your body's rate of heat loss is frequently greater than its rate of heat production. Under these conditions, hypothermia may result. You can help prevent heat stress illnesses and hypothermia by following certain precautions.

Planning your fitness program involves setting your fitness goals and designing your fitness program so that it is best suited to your needs.

Learning Objectives

1. Describe the benefits of physical activity, including improved cardiorespiratory efficiency, skeletal mass, weight control, health and life span, mental health and stress management, and physical fitness.

2. Describe the components of an aerobic exercise program and how to determine proper exercise frequency, intensity, and duration.

3. Describe the different stretching exercises designed to improve flexibility.

4. Compare the various types of resistance training programs, including the methods of providing external resistance and intended physiological benefits.

5. Describe common fitness injuries, suggest ways to prevent injuries, and list the treatment process.

6. Summarize the key components of a personal fitness program.

Key Terms

Fill in a brief definition to help you remember these terms.

systolic blood pressure _____

diastolic blood pressure_____

osteoarthritis _____

osteoporosis_____

physical fitness _____

exercise _____

exercise training _____

cardiovascular fitness _____

aerobic fitness_____

aerobic capacity_____

graded exercise test _____

target heart rate _____

flexibility_____

static stretching _____

muscular strength _____

one repetition maximum (1RM) _____

muscular endurance _____

resistance exercise program _____

hypertrophy _____

isometric muscle action _____

concentric muscle action _____

eccentric muscle action _____

overuse injuries _____

traumatic injuries _____

RICE _____

heat cramps _____

heat exhaustion _____

heat stroke _____

hypothermia _____

cross training _____

Critical Thinking Exercises

1. Alayna has just begun a regular exercise program at a fitness centre. What psychological benefits can she expect to gain by engaging in regular physical activity?

2. David is 35 years old. He is monitoring his exercise intensity during aerobic exercise. David wants to exercise at 70 percent of his maximum heart rate. What is his target heart rate? How can David determine how close he is to this value during his workout?

3. What activity could you engage in to apply body weight resistance? Fixed resistance? Variable resistance? Accommodating resistance?

4. Andre sprained his ankle during a one-on-one basketball game. Explain how to apply the first-aid treatment known as RICE to Andre's ankle.

Critical Thinking Activity: Planning My Personal Fitness Program

Plan your own fitness program. Use the following worksheet to help you design a fitness program that meets your individual needs.

PLANNING MY PERSONAL FITNESS PROGRAM

What is my primary reason for exercising?

What are my fitness goals?

What type of fitness program is best suited to my needs? (What amount of exercise? What type of exercise?)

Do I need to consult my physician before I begin my fitness program?

What exercise clothing and equipment do I need?

Good fitness programs are designed to improve or maintain fitness in all four major components. What will I include in my comprehensive program?

The following schedule is what I choose for an exercise program:

Sunday

• Type of exercise	
• Frequency of exercise	
• Duration of exercise	
• Location of exercise	

Monday

• Type of exercise	
• Frequency of exercise	
• Duration of exercise	
• Location of exercise	

Tuesday

• Type of exercise	
• Frequency of exercise	
• Duration of exercise	
• Location of exercise	

Wednesday

• Type of exercise	
• Frequency of exercise	
• Duration of exercise	
• Location of exercise	

Thursday

• Type of exercise	
• Frequency of exercise	
• Duration of exercise	
• Location of exercise	

Friday

• Type of exercise	
• Frequency of exercise	
• Duration of exercise	
• Location of exercise	

Saturday

• Type of exercise	
• Frequency of exercise	
• Duration of exercise	
• Location of exercise	

General Review Questions

Short Answer

1. What is an effective method for losing weight?

2. List six physiological benefits of regular exercise.

3. Name the four components of physical fitness.

4. What are the three components of aerobic fitness programs?

5. What are three principles for improving muscular strength?

6. Identify and define the three types of muscle activity.

7. What are three common overuse injuries?

8. What first-aid treatment can be used for virtually all physical fitness related injuries?

Multiple Choice

1. The leading cause of death in Canada for both men and women is:
   a. Cancer
   b. Strokes
   c. Coronary heart disease
   d. Liver disease

2. The ability of the heart, lungs, and blood vessels to function efficiently is called:
   a. Cardiovascular output
   b. Cardiovascular status
   c. Cardiovascular fitness
   d. Cardiovascular endurance

3. A test of aerobic capacity administered by a physician, exercise physiologist, or other trained person is called:
   a. A graded exercise test
   b. A maximum aerobic capacity test
   c. An aerobic endurance test
   d. A cardiac output test

4. The length of a daily physical activity of exercise period to improve aerobic capacity is:
   a. No more than 10 minutes
   b. 10-15 minutes
   c. 15-20 minutes
   d. 20-60 minutes

5. A regular program of exercise designed to improve muscular strength and endurance in the major muscle groups is:
   a. Flexibility training program
   b. Aerobic exercise program
   c. Repetition maximum program
   d. Resistance exercise program

6. An Indian form of exercise widely practiced in the West today that promotes balance, coordination, flexibility and meditation is:
   a. Flexibility
   b. Tai chi
   c. Yoga
   d. Zen

7. The greatest amount of force in the muscles is produced during:
   a. Muscle overload
   b. Isometric muscle action
   c. Concentric muscle action
   d. Eccentric muscle actions

8. The primary category of physical activity known to improve cardiovascular fitness is:
   a. Aerobic exercise
   b. Anaerobic exercise
   c. Flexibility
   d. Body building

9. The type of muscle action in which force is produced while the muscle shortens is called:
   a. Dynamic
   b. Static
   c. Concentric
   d. Eccentric

10. The resistance provided by exercises that require your muscles to lift your body weight off the floor (i.e. situps, pushups, pullups) is called:
    a. Fixed resistance
    b. Variable resistance
    c. Accommodating resistance
    d. Body weight resistance

11. The general term for any pain that occurs below the knee and above the ankle is:
    a. Shin splints
    b. Tendonitis
    c. Muscle cramps
    d. Muscle strain

12. Superior stretching techniques that are best performed with a certified athletic trainer or physical therapist are called:
    a. Static stretching techniques
    b. Proprioceptive neuromuscular facilitation
    c. Ballistic stretching techniques
    d. Tandem stretching techniques

13. The amount of force a muscle is capable of exerting is:
    a. Muscular efficiency
    b. Muscular strength
    c. Muscular endurance
    d. Muscular overload

14. The use of free-weight barbells and dumbbells that offer a resistance to your exertion is an example of:
    a. Body weight resistance
    b. Fixed resistance
    c. Variable resistance
    d. Static resistance

15. A condition in which the body's rate of heat production exceeds its ability to cool itself is known as:
    a. Hypothermia
    b. Heat stress
    c. Compression
    d. Muscle strain

16. People who exercise regularly often report:
    a. An increased ability to cope with stress
    b. An increased self-esteem
    c. Feeling good about personal appearance
    d. All of the above

17. Muscle endurance is:
    a. The force exerted by a muscle that is less than or equal to the resistance
    b. A muscle's ability to exert force repeatedly without fatiguing
    c. The length of time a particular movement can be sustained by a muscle or muscle group
    d. A withering of muscle tissue that can result from injury or disease

18. The strongest predisposing factor for non-insulin dependent diabetes is(are):
    a. Obesity
    b. Increasing age
    c. Family history of diabetes
    d. All of the above

19. The systematic performance of exercise at a specified frequency, intensity, and duration to achieve a desired level of physical fitness is called:
    a. Fitness training
    b. Physical fitness
    c. Exercise training
    d. Physical endurance

20. Force produced while lengthening the muscle is called:
    a. Eccentric muscle action
    b. Isotonic muscle action
    c. Concentric muscle action
    d. Endurance muscle action

21. The recommended minimum number of times per week that a physical activity and/or exercise should be done to reach aerobic fitness is:
    a. 1 time per week
    b. 3 times per week
    c. 5 times per week
    d. 7 times per week

22. Increased levels of high density lipoproteins can diminish the risk of:
    a. Diabetes
    b. Osteoarthritis
    c. Osteoporosis
    d. Cardiovascular disease

23. Which of the following is(are) warning signs of overuse injury?
    a. Muscle stiffness
    b. Whole body fatigue
    c. Joint pain
    d. All of the above

24. The type of resistance that provides a "constant load" on the muscle throughout the entire range of motion is called:
    a. Body weight resistance
    b. Static resistance
    c. Fixed resistance
    d. Accommodating resistance

25. The use of resistance that is altered throughout the range of motion so that the effort by the muscle is more consistent throughout the full range of motion is called:
    a. Static resistance
    b. Muscular function resistance
    c. Variable resistance
    d. Isometric resistance

26. The maximal volume of oxygen consumed by muscles during exercise is:
    a. Flexibility
    b. Muscle endurance
    c. Aerobic capacity
    d. Maximum oxygen capacity

27. To lose weight, how many workouts a week will you need to do in order to see reductions in your total body mass and fat mass?
    a. At least 2 workouts per week
    b. At least 3 workouts per week
    c. At least 4 workouts per week
    d. At least 5 workouts per week

28. Injuries that result from the cumulative effects of day-after-day stress placed on tendons, muscles, and joints are called:
    a. Overuse injuries
    b. Traumatic injuries
    c. Overtraining injuries
    d. Repetitive injuries

29. Joel enjoys various types of fitness exercises. He alternates his training days with jogging, cycling, and step aerobics. This type of training is called:
    a. Cardiac fitness training
    b. Static training
    c. Cross training
    d. Multisport training

30. Techniques to gradually lengthen a muscle to an elongated position (to the point of discomfort) and hold that position for 10 to 30 seconds is called:
    a. Dynamic stretching
    b. Static stretching
    c. Variable stretching
    d. Concentric stretching

Language Enrichment Glossary

In addition to the words in the Key Terms list at the end of the chapter, students listed the following words as difficult to understand. Use the chapter Key Terms list, this list, your dictionary, and teachers and friends to learn the meaning of words you do not understand.

absorbency:	ability to absorb
accelerating:	speed up
acclimatization:	becoming used to
accommodate:	fit
accumulate:	gather
adequate:	enough
afflicted:	to suffer from
alters:	changes
apathy:	inactivity, disinterest
arch:	raised middle of sole of foot
attain:	to reach
barbell:	a heavy exercise weight
bouts:	periods
briskly:	actively
cadence:	pattern
colon:	intestine
compartments:	parts
component:	part
concept:	idea
coronary:	heart
curl:	lifting weights, reducing angle between two bones
current:	up-to-date
customizes:	adjusts to fit
debilitating:	weakening
desire:	strong want
despair:	to give up
detrimental:	harmful
dumbbell:	exercise weight
duration:	period of time
efficiency:	smooth, not wasteful
elongation:	to make longer
embark:	begin
endurance:	ability to last for a long time
exerted:	applied
exertion:	effort
expenditure:	payment
external:	outside
extremities:	arms and legs
facets:	sides
facial:	on the face

fatiguing:	tiring
flexed:	bent
flexion:	angle decreasing movement at a hinge joint
goggles:	protective glasses
goosebumps:	skin bumps caused by feeling cold or scared
hard task:	difficult job
immersion:	covered by water
initiating:	starting
integral:	central
intensity:	power
interdependent:	affect each other
levelled off:	stopped increasing
light:	not much, not heavy
load:	burden, amount of work
midsole:	middle of shoe sole
moderate:	medium
modes:	ways
monotonous:	repetitive, boring
nonfatal:	doesn't cause death
novice:	newcomer, minimal knowledge or experience
obesity:	overweight
osteoporosis:	bone deterioration
overload:	too large a burden
padded grips:	padding on handles
paradoxically:	contradictory
portability:	easy to carry
postures:	way of holding the body
predictor:	estimate
prevalent:	common
prudent:	careful
receptors:	receivers
resiliency:	adaptability, flexibility
retention:	holding
reusable:	can be used repeatedly
sampling:	trying
segment:	part
sequential:	step by step
squats:	bending at the knees while in a standing position
stemming:	coming from
susceptible:	a tendency toward
sustain:	maintain
systematic:	organized
tension:	force, pulling
treadmill:	stationary walking device for exercise
vigorous:	strong, active

CHAPTER 10
Licit and Illicit Drug Use Understanding Addictions

Chapter Overview

Addiction is defined as patterned use that carries with it a dependence on mind or mood altering substances which has attained such a degree as to disrupt academic or work performance, interfere with family and interpersonal relationships, disrupt social and economic functioning and impair the state of physical and/or mental health. All addictions are characterized by compulsion, loss of control, negative consequences, and denial. Addiction is a process that evolves over time.

Drugs are chemical substances with the potential to alter the structure and function of our bodies. Scientists divide drugs into six categories prescription drugs, over-the-counter preparations, recreational substances, herbal preparations, illicit drugs, and commercial drugs. The way in which a given drug is taken into the body is called the route of administration. Common routes are oral ingestion, injection, inhalation, inunction, and suppository.

The use of a drug for a purpose for which it was not intended is called drug misuse. Drug abuse is the excessive use of any drug. The misuse and abuse of drugs may lead to addiction. Creating a drug profile before you decide whether to use a chemical substance can help you intelligently weigh the risks and benefits of a particular drug. Individuals respond differently to psychoactive drugs. Two environmental factors that bear on both the main effects and the side effects of psychoactive drugs are set and setting. Set is the total internal environment, or mindset, of a person at the time a drug is taken, while the setting refers to the external environment of a person at the time a drug is taken. Polydrug use, or taking several medications or illegal drugs simultaneously, may cause very dangerous problems associated with drug interactions. The most hazardous interactions are synergism, antagonism, inhibition, and intolerance. Hazardous interactions may also occur between drugs and nutrients.

Prescription drugs are administered under medical supervision. Types of prescription drugs include antibiotics, analgesics, sedatives, tranquilizers, antidepressants, and amphetamines. Generic drugs are medications sold under their chemical name and contain the same active ingredients as their brand-name counterparts.

Over-the-counter (OTC) drugs are those nonprescription drugs we use in the course of self-diagnosis and self-medication. The most commonly used over-the-counter drugs are analgesics, cold/cough/allergy and asthma relievers, stimulants, sleeping aids and relaxants, and dieting aids.

Illicit drugs are illegal to possess, produce, and sell. Although the use of illicit drugs has seen a significant decline in recent years, usage is still quite high. Drug control programs have been developed to deal with the problems of illegal drug use. The major drawback of most of these programs has been their failure to take a multidimensional approach.

In order to combat the growing problem of illegal drug use and the overuse of certain prescription drugs, Parliament passed the Controlled Drugs and Substances Act of 1996. This law created categories for both prescription and illegal substances for which the federal government required strict regulation. Hundreds of illegal drugs exist. For general purposes, they can be divided into five categories stimulants, marijuana and its derivatives, depressants, psychedelics and deliriants, and designer drugs. Cocaine is a crystallized white alkaloid powder derived from the leaves of the South American coca shrub. It is a very dangerous stimulant that can be taken in several ways"snorted" through the nose, smoked, or intravenous injections. The amphetamines include a large and varied group of synthetic agents that stimulate the central nervous system. Newer-generation stimulants include crank and ice. Marijuana is the most extensively used illicit drug by far. The long-term use of marijuana causes lung damage comparable to that caused by tobacco smoking. Marijuana has been used to control the side effects of chemotherapy and to reduce the symptoms of glaucoma. Opiates cause drowsiness, relieve pain, and induce euphoria. Besides opium, they include morphine, codeine, heroin, and black tar heroin. Opiates are powerful central nervous system depressants, lowering heart rate, respiration, and blood pressure. Treatments for addiction to opiates have not been very successful. Methadone maintenance is controversial because of its addictive potential. Psychedelics are a group of drugs whose primary effect is to alter feelings, perceptions, and thoughts in the user. One psychedelic, lysergic acid diethylamide (LSD), is one of the most powerful drugs known to science. Deliriants produce confusion and disorientation at relatively low doses. Phencyclidine (PCP) is the best-known deliriant. Designer drugs are structural analogs of drugs already included under the Controlled Drugs and Substances Act. These illegal drugs are manufactured by underground chemists to mimic the psychoactive effects of controlled drugs. Synthetic drugs available on the illegal drug market include analogs of PCP, analogs of fentanyl and meperidine, and analogs of amphetamine and methamphetamine. Inhalants are chemicals that produce hallucinogenic vapours, such as rubber cement, model glue, paint thinner, and lighter fluid. Anabolic steroids are artificial forms of the male hormone testosterone that produce muscle growth and strength. Several adverse effects occur in those who use steroids. They cause mood swings, acne, liver tumours, elevated cholesterol levels, hypertension, kidney disease, and immune system disturbances. There is also a danger of AIDS transmission through shared needles.

Illicit drugs cost the Canadian economy $1.4 billion in 1996. Female addicts have special problems associated with seeking treatment. Estimates are that 30 percent of the population have used illicit drugs at some point. The use of mandatory drug urinalysis is controversial.

Researchers agree that a multimodal approach to drug education is best. Factual information works better than scare tactics. The best answer is education and self-discipline.

Learning Objectives

1. Distinguish addictions from habits and identify the signs of addiction.
2. List the six categories of drugs and explain the routes of administration that drugs take into the body.
3. Discuss proper drug use and explain how hazardous drug interactions occur.
4. Discuss the types of over-the-counter drugs and general precautions to be taken with them.
5. Discuss the key questions you should ask in order to make intelligent decisions about drug use.
6. Discuss patterns of illicit drug use, including who uses illicit drugs and why they use them.
7. Describe the use and abuse of controlled substances, including cocaine, amphetamines, marijuana, opiates, psychedelics, deliriants, designer drugs, and inhalants.
8. Profile overall illegal drug use in Canada, including frequency, financial impact, arrests for drug offenses, and impact on the workplace.

Key Terms

Fill in a brief definition to help you remember these terms.

addiction _____

withdrawal _____

relapse _____

compulsion _____

obsession _____

loss of control _____

negative consequences _____

denial _____

nurturing through avoidance _____

neurotransmitters _____

tolerance _____

receptor sites _____

psychoactive drugs _____

prescription drugs _____

over-the-counter (OTC) drugs _____

recreational drugs _____

herbal preparations _____

illicit (illegal) drugs _____

commercial preparations _____

route of administration _____

oral ingestion _____

injection _____

intravenous injection _____

intramuscular injection _____

subcutaneous injection _____

inhalation _____

inunction _____

suppositories _____

drug misuse _____

drug abuse _____

set _____

setting _____

polydrug use _____

synergism _____

antagonism _____

inhibition _____

intolerance _____

cross-tolerance _____

antibiotics _____

analgesics _____

prostaglandin inhibitors _____

sedatives _____

tranquilizers _____

antidepressants _____

amphetamines _____

rebound effects _____

generic drugs _____

sympathomimetics _____

98

laxative _____

diuretic _____

illicit drugs _____

cocaine _____

freebase _____

crack _____

crank _____

ice _____

marijuana_____

tetrahydrocannabinol (THC) _____

hashish_____

narcotics _____

opium _____

morphine _____

codeine _____

heroin _____

black tar heroin _____

endorphins_____

methadone maintenance _____

psychedelics _____

reticular formation_____

synesthesia _____

hallucination _____

lysergic acid diethylamide (LSD) _____

mescaline_____

peyote _____

psilocybin _____

delirium _____

deliriant _____

phencyclidine (PCP) _____

designer drug_____

inhalants _____

amyl nitrite _____

nitrous oxide _____

anabolic steroids _____

erogenic drug_____

Critical Thinking Exercises

1. Lyle, your friend from high school, is staying with you while going through a divorce. He likes to drink alcohol, and now you see that he has prescription barbiturates to help him sleep. What concern do you have about Lyle mixing alcohol and barbiturates?

2. Ann takes ibuprofen, a prostaglandin inhibitor, for her menstrual cramps. How does this drug work?

3. Your friend, Kayla, has been using prescription amphetamines for several months to treat obesity. Now she is ready to quit. What rebound effects might she experience?

4. Your friend is sick and asks you to pick up her prescription drugs at the pharmacy. She asks your advice about using a generic form of the drug. What do you tell her?

5. Your friend, Laura, has been using laxatives and diuretics to lose weight and she brags that she has lost two dress sizes, seeking your approval. What do you say to her about the health consequences of her actions?

6. Theo entered a drug treatment program for cocaine use. In group therapy, he disclosed that he "shot up" cocaine. The group members shared their concerns for Theo's health. What are their concerns about his risk for infection and disease?

Critical Thinking Activity: Your Safe and Responsible Use of Prescription Drugs

Visiting a physician does not exempt you from exercising responsibility for your own health. Too often, individuals simply take the prescription medication without asking basic questions about the medication and just assume that the doctor knows best. Answer the following questions about your pattern of prescription drug use.

1. I take prescription drugs.

    Always   Usually   Sometimes   Rarely   Never

2. I ask questions about why I am being given a specific prescription.

    Always   Usually   Sometimes   Rarely   Never

3. I inform the doctor or pharmacist of any allergies to medications.

    Always   Usually   Sometimes   Rarely   Never

4. I know the side effects of the prescription drugs that I take.

    Always   Usually   Sometimes   Rarely   Never

5. I know the benefits of the prescription drugs I take.

    Always   Usually   Sometimes   Rarely   Never

6. I know how my prescription drug should be administered.

    Always   Usually   Sometimes   Rarely   Never

7. I know about whether my prescription drug is available as a generic drug.

    Always   Usually   Sometimes   Rarely   Never

8. I have rejected my doctor's recommendation regarding medication.

    Always   Usually   Sometimes   Rarely   Never

9. I take my prescription drug as instructed.

    Always   Usually   Sometimes   Rarely   Never

Questions for the Critical Thinker

After you have completed this exercise, reflect on the following questions. Your thoughtful responses will enhance your learning of this activity as well as your knowledge of pharmaceutical drugs.

1. What do your answers suggest about how good a consumer you are when it comes to medication?
2. How much responsibility have you assumed for your use of prescription drugs?
3. What do you need to improve, if anything?
4. Do you think your level of consumerism is typical?

General Review Questions

Short Answer

1. In order for a behaviour to be addictive, what potential must a behaviour have?
2. Identify four components that are present in all addictions.
3. List three examples of a recreational drug.
4. Name the five common routes of administration of drugs.
5. What is the difference between drug misuse and drug abuse?
6. Define synergism. When is a synergistic interaction most likely to occur?

Multiple Choice

1. Drugs work by:
    a. Interfering with the body's processes
    b. Short circuiting the body and redirecting the chemicals that are produced abnormally
    c. Resembling physically the chemicals produced naturally within the body
    d. Reducing the amount of chemicals that are produced at abnormally high rates

2. Alcohol, tobacco, caffeine, tea, and chocolate products are categorized as:
    a. Over-the-counter drugs
    b. Recreational drugs
    c. Herbal preparations
    d. Illicit drugs

3. Antibiotics and vaccinations are normally administered by:
    a. Intramuscular injection
    b. Inhalation
    c. Intravenous injection
    d. Suppositories

4. Administration of a drug through the nostrils is called:
    a. Oral ingestion
    b. Intravenous injection
    c. Inhalation
    d. Inunction

5. Taking a drug for a longer time or more often than is intended is an example of:
    a. Drug abuse
    b. Drug misuse
    c. Synergistic drug use
    d. Illicit drug use

6. Rebecca takes a number of medications for various medical conditions, including prinivil (an antihypertensive), insulin (a diabetic medication), and claridin (an antihistamine). This is an example of:
    a. Synergism
    b. Illegal drug use
    c. Polydrug use
    d. Antagonism

7. When a person develops a physiological tolerance to one drug and shows a similar tolerance to selected other drugs as a result, it is known as:
   a. Synergism
   b. Antagonism
   c. Cross-tolerance
   d. Polydrug use

8. The less-powerful tranquilizers used in the treatment of psychiatric illnesses are called:
   a. Analgesics
   b. Antidepressants
   c. Minor tranquilizers
   d. Major tranquilizers

9. The type of interaction in which the effects of one drug are eliminated or reduced by the presence of another drug at the receptor site is called:
   a. Antagonism
   b. Cross-tolerance
   c. Intolerance
   d. Inhibition

10. Which of the following medicines can keep birth control pills from working and result in an accidental pregnancy?
    a. Penicillin
    b. Tuberculosis medicines
    c. Anxiety medicines
    d. All of the above

11. Drugs that are used to relieve pain are classified as:
    a. Analgesics
    b. Antibiotics
    c. Depressants
    d. Psychoactives

12. Amphetamines:
    a. Cause elevated blood pressure
    b. Suppress appetite
    c. Adversely affect respiration
    d. All of the above

13. To reduce the incidence of problems from OTC drug use, it is important to:
    a. Always know what you are taking by identifying the active ingredient(s) in the product
    b. Read the warnings and cautions
    c. Don't use anything for more than one or two weeks
    d. All of the above

14. It is spring and Roy is experiencing allergy symptoms, including a runny nose, sinus congestion, and tearing. When he goes to the store to buy an over-the-counter preparation, Roy would most likely buy a(n):
    a. Decongestant
    b. Expectorant
    c. Antihistamine
    d. Antitussive

15. Herbal products are unique because:
    a. Their active ingredients have little or no federal regulation
    b. Their ingredients are natural and harness
    c. They are safe due to thousands of years of use without any complications
    d. They can be purchased without a prescription

16. Drugs with a high potential for abuse and addiction and have no medical use are categorized as:
    a. Schedule I drugs
    b. Schedule II drugs
    c. Schedule III drugs
    d. Schedule IV drugs

17. A potent, inexpensive stimulant that has long-lasting effects is:
    a. Caffeine
    b. Nicotine
    c. Cocaine
    d. " Ice"

18. "Snorting" cocaine through the nose can cause all of the following physical effects, except:
    a. Damage to the mucous membranes in the nose and sinusitis
    b. Severely damaged liver disease
    c. Destroy the user's sense of smell
    d. Creates a hole in the septum

19. A derivative of opium that is sometimes used to relieve pain is:
    a. Morphine
    b. Heroin
    c. Codeine
    d. Methadone

20. The sticky resin of the marijuana plant is called:
    a. Ghanja
    b. Hashish
    c. Black tar
    d. Cannabis sativa

21. Marijuana has been used in the medical treatment of:
    a. Glaucoma
    b. Cancer chemotherapy
    c. Diabetes
    d. Both a and b

22. The narcotic used in cough syrups and certain painkillers is:
    a. Morphine
    b. Cocaine
    c. Codeine
    d. Heroin

23. The most common route of administration for heroin addicts is:
    a. Inhalation
    b. Intravenous injection
    c. Ingestion
    d. Transdermal

24. Opiate-like hormones that are manufactured in the human brain and contribute to feelings of well-being are:
    a. Endorphins

b. Acetaminaphine
c. Adrenaline
d. Acetylcholine

25. The group of drugs whose primary pharmacological effect is characterized by confusion and disorientation in the user is:
    a. Narcotics
    b. Deliriants
    c. Stimulants
    d. Depressants

26. The fastest growing illicit drug among the under 22 age group is:
    a. Black tar heroin
    b. Crack cocaine
    c. LSD
    d. Ecstasy

27. A hallucinogenic drug derived from the peyote cactus is:
    a. Mescaline
    b. Methamphetamine
    c. LSD
    d. Psilocybin

28. An example of a deliriant drug is:
    a. Tetrahydrocannabinol (THC)
    b. Phencyclidine (PCP)
    c. Ecstasy (MDMA)
    d. Lysergic Acid Diethylamide (LSD)

29. MPTP, a street analog of heroin, has been known to cause an irreversible brain syndrome similar to:
    a. Alzheimer's disease
    b. Huntington's disease
    c. Parkinson's disease
    d. Korsakoff's syndrome

30. The effects of nitrous oxide include all of the following except:
    a. Pain relief
    b. Giggling
    c. Skin flushing
    d. Euphoria

Language Enrichment Glossary

In addition to the words in the Key Terms list at the end of the chapter, students listed the following words as difficult to understand. Use the chapter Key Terms list, this list, your dictionary, and teachers and friends to learn the meaning of words you do not understand.

accelerated:	speeded up
adhesive patches:	sticky skin pad containing chemicals
adjunct:	addition
adverse:	negative
affinity:	attraction to
alleviate:	lessen
analgesics:	pain-killers
analogs:	similar substances
anesthetics:	painkillers
antacid:	product reducing stomach acid pain
antisocial:	unfriendly, hostile to others
atrophy:	deteriorate, shrink to smaller size
attributable to:	caused by
benign:	good or harmless
binds:	attaches to
bizarre:	very strange
caught up:	involved in
coma:	unconscious condition
compile:	gather, collect
complement:	addition to
concerted:	strong
concoctions:	mixtures
constipation:	difficulty moving bowels
contend:	say, believe
controversy:	disagreement, conflict
corrosive:	causes erosion or deterioration
cravings:	desires
cultivation:	encourage to grow, develop
curtail:	limit, reduce
definitive:	absolute, definite
deliriants:	chemicals causing confusion, unconsciousness
dependence:	need to have something, addiction
depletion:	reduction of, loss of
derivatives:	something that came from something else
diminish:	reduce
dispensed:	distributed
dispersion:	spread throughout
disrupts:	disturbs, interrupts
derivative:	substance made from something else
derived:	developed from

dilapidated:	broken down, worn out
dilation:	opening up
directives:	rules, orders
dissolution:	dissolving, breaking apart
emerge:	develop, become visible
endorphins:	body chemicals which cause good feelings
enhance:	to intensify or increase
entailed:	involved
erroneously:	incorrectly
exhibit:	show
exhorting:	trying to convince
fatigue:	tiredness
fetus:	unborn baby
giddy:	dizzy, silly
hallucinations:	imagined visions which seem real
hence:	therefore, because of this
hurdles:	barriers
hypodermic syringe:	needle and plunger to inject something
illicit:	illegal
inconclusive:	no conclusion
ingrown nails:	nails which grow painfully into the skin
instituted:	started
intravenous:	in the veins
introspective:	looking inward to the self
joint:	marijuana cigarette
justified:	done with good reason
metabolized:	chemical process of being absorbed into and used by the body
mimic:	imitate
mood-altering:	changes emotional states
multimodal:	using may ways
nauseated:	stomach upset
neglected:	not paid attention to
negligible:	very small, unimportant
nostalgia:	good memories of the past
notorious:	negatively well-known
obligations:	commitments, responsibilities
opium poppy:	flower containing opium
pales:	is minor, not as important
percolating:	dripping
phenomenon:	occurrence, event
physiology:	biological process
possess:	have, contain
prescribed:	recommended by a doctor
prevails:	succeeds
proponents:	those who agree with

remedies:	treatments
relevant:	appropriate, related to
resemble:	similar to
resolved:	settled
rush:	rapid good feeling
sanctioned:	approved
shoots up:	injects
snorts:	sniffs
spores:	tiny, single-cell seeds
surpassed:	greater than
syndrome:	group of symptoms of medical condition
synthetic:	made by humans, not natural
unforeseeable:	unexpected
unspectacular:	not outstanding, unsuccessful
universally:	everywhere
waxy medium:	wax used to mix with
viable:	realistic
volatile:	explodes easily

CHAPTER 11
Alcohol, Tobacco, and Caffeine Unacknowledged Addictions

Chapter Overview

As a society, we refuse to categorize alcohol as a drug because it is socially accepted, but alcohol is the most used, and abused, recreational drug in our society. An estimated 58 percent of Canadians consume alcoholic beverages regularly. Alcohol is used on university and college campuses to relieve tensions and to celebrate. But it is also used to escape negative feelings, to release unacceptable emotions, or simply to get drunk. Our society condones, approves, and often encourages the consumption of alcoholic beverages, but neglects to teach us how to use alcohol responsibly.

Behavioural changes caused by alcohol vary with the set and setting and with the individual. Blood alcohol concentration (B.A.C.) is used to measure the physiological and behavioural effects of alcohol. How quickly the body absorbs alcohol is influenced by several factors, including the alcohol concentration in the drink, the amount of alcohol consumed, the amount of food in your stomach, and your mood. A drinker's blood alcohol content also depends on weight and body fat, the water content in body tissues, the rate of consumption, and the volume of alcohol consumed. Women have half as much of the enzyme that breaks down alcohol in the stomach. Therefore if a man and a woman both drink the same amount of alcohol, the woman's blood alcohol content will be 30 percent higher than the man's. The most dramatic immediate effects produced by alcohol occur in the central nervous system, leading to decreases in respiratory rate, pulse, and blood pressure. In extreme cases, coma and death can result. A hangover is often experienced the morning after a drinking spree. Chronic alcohol consumption can have serious cumulative effects, including effects on the nervous system, cardiovascular effects, liver disease, and cancer. Fetal alcohol syndrome is associated with alcohol consumption throughout pregnancy. Among fatally injured drivers, 42 percent had some alcohol in their blood.

Alcohol use turns into alcohol abuse or alcoholism when it interferes with work, school, social or family relationships, or when it entails any violation of the law. Ninety-five percent of alcoholics live in some type of extended family unit. They can be found at all levels of society. Women are the fastest-growing component of the population of alcohol abusers. Alcohol is a disease with biological, psychological, and social/environmental components. A family history of alcoholism may predispose a person to problems with alcohol. Certain social factors have been linked to alcoholism, including urbanization, the weakening of links to the extended family, increased mobility, and changing religious and philosophical values. The alcoholic's entire family suffers from the disease of alcoholism. The entire society also suffers the consequences of individuals' alcohol abuse. The annual cost of alcohol abuse to society is estimated at $7.5 billion in 1996.

An intervention is an effective method of helping an alcoholic to confront the disease. An alcoholic can get treatment from private treatment facilities, family therapy, individual therapy, group therapy, drug and aversion therapy, or Alcoholics Anonymous. Roughly 60 percent of alcoholics relapse within the first three months of treatment. Treating an addiction requires not only getting the addict to stop using, but it also requires the person to break a pattern of behaviour that has dominated his or her life.

The single most preventable cause of death in Canada is the use of tobacco. According to the Statistics Canada 28.6 percent of males and females smoke. Tobacco companies spend billions of dollars in advertising, and because children and teenagers make up 85 percent of all new smokers, much of the advertising has been directed at them. The use of tobacco products is costly to all of us in terms of lost productivity and lost lives.

Tobacco is sold in several forms cigarettes, cigars, pipes, snuff, and chewing tobacco. The chemical stimulant nicotine is the major psychoactive substance in all these tobacco products. Nicotine is a powerful central nervous system stimulant that produces an aroused, alert mental state. Nicotine also stimulates the adrenal glands, increasing the production of adrenaline. The physical effects of nicotine stimulation include increased heart and respiratory rate, constriction of blood vessels, and subsequent increased blood pressure. Nicotine decreases the stomach contractions that signal hunger, decreases blood sugar levels, and decreases the sensation in the taste buds.

Tobacco smoking has been directly linked to cancer, cardiovascular disease, strokes, respiratory diseases, and gum disease. Female smokers have a greater risk of developing cervical cancer and heart disease than do female nonsmokers. Women who smoke and use oral contraceptives run a higher risk of stroke and heart attack. Smoking also appears to cause women to begin menopause prematurely and contributes to osteoporosis. Cigarette smoking presents special dangers for pregnant women and their fetuses, including miscarriages, low birthweights, higher infant mortality rates, and higher rates of sudden infant death syndrome.

There are two types of smokeless tobacco — chewing tobacco and snuff. Smokeless tobacco is just as addictive as cigarettes due to its nicotine content. In fact, smokeless tobacco has more nicotine than cigarettes. One of the major risks of chewing tobacco is leucoplakia, which can develop into oral cancer.

Environmental tobacco smoke is divided into two categories mainstream smoke and sidestream smoke. Involuntary smokers face risks from exposure to tobacco smoke because secondhand smoke actually contains more carcinogenic substances than the smoke that a smoker inhales. Efforts to ban smoking have gained momentum in recent years as municipalities look to pass by-laws restricting smoking.

Quitting smoking is difficult. There are a variety of methods to help the smoker quit, including nicotine chewing gum, the nicotine patch, aversion therapy, operant conditioning, and self-control therapy. There are numerous health benefits of quitting smoking. For instance, at the end of 10 smoke-free years, the ex-smoker can expect to live out his or her normal life span.

Caffeine is a drug derived from the chemical family called xanthines, which are mild central nervous system stimulants that enhance mental alertness and reduce fatigue. Side effects of xanthines include wakefulness, insomnia, irregular heartbeat, dizziness, nausea, indigestion, and sometimes mild delirium. Caffeinism is caffeine intoxication caused by excessive caffeine use, with symptoms including chronic insomnia, jitters, irritability, nervousness, anxiety, and involuntary muscle twitches. Moderate caffeine consumption produces very few harmful effects in healthy, nonpregnant people.

Learning Objectives

1. Summarize the alcohol use patterns of university and college students and discuss overall trends in consumption.
2. Explain the physiological and behavioural effects of alcohol, including blood alcohol concentration, absorption, metabolism, and immediate and long-term effects of alcohol consumption.
3. Explain the symptoms and causes of alcoholism, its cost to society, and its effects on the family.
4. Explain the treatment of alcoholism, including the family's role, varied treatment methods, and whether or not alcoholics can be cured.

5.   Discuss the social issues involved in tobacco use, including advertising and the health care costs associated with tobacco use.

6.   Review how smoking affects a smoker's risk for cancer, cardiovascular disease, and respiratory diseases, and how it adversely affects the health of a fetus.

7.   Discuss the risks associated with using smokeless tobacco.

8.   Evaluate the risks to nonsmokers associated with environmental tobacco smoke.

9.   Describe strategies people adopt to quit using tobacco products, including strategies aimed at breaking the nicotine addiction as well as the habit.

10. Compare the benefits and risks associated with caffeine, and summarize the health consequences of long-term caffeine use.

Key Terms

Fill in a brief definition to help you remember these terms.

binge drinking _____

ethyl alcohol (ethanol)_____

fermentation _____

distillation _____

proof _____

blood-alcohol concentration (BAC) _____

learned behavioural tolerance _____

dehydration _____

cerebrospinal fluid_____

hangover _____

congeners _____

cirrhosis_____

alcohol hepatitis _____

fetal alcohol syndrome (FAS) _____

fetal alcohol effects (FAE) _____

alcohol abuse (alcoholism) _____

intervention _____

delirium tremens (Dts) _____

Alcoholics Anonymous _____

snuff _____

chewing tobacco _____

nicotine _____

tar _____

carbon monoxide _____

nicotine poisoning _____

platelet adhesiveness _____

emphysema _____

sudden infant death syndrome (SIDS) _____

leucoplakia _____

environmental tobacco smoke (ETS) _____

mainstream smoke _____

sidestream smoke _____

nicotine withdrawal _____

caffeine _____

xanthines _____

caffeinism _____

Critical Thinking Exercises

1. Suppose you have been asked to present a lecture on the long-term effects of alcohol consumption to patients in a treatment recovery program. What long-term effects would you address?

2. Nancy lives in a dysfunctional family. Her father is an alcoholic and compulsive gambler. Nancy diverts attention away from her father by refusing to eat at family meals, exercising excessively, and losing a significant amount of weight. Nancy's anorexic behaviours may be the result of assuming what role in her family?

3. Jonah is an alcoholic. After an intervention involving his family members and a therapist, he has agreed to enter a treatment program. When he does quit drinking, what withdrawal symptoms is he most likely to experience?

4. Your friend, Edna, finally listens to your warnings about the dangers of tobacco smoking. She tells you that after giving it much thought, she is switching to clove cigarettes. How would you react? Why?

5. Cindy and Liz are best friends, but Cindy's smoking really bothers Liz. When Liz asks Cindy not to smoke when they are together, Cindy says, "I'm only hurting myself, not you." Is she correct? Why or why not?

6. Your mother has been a very heavy coffee drinker for several years. Now she has reduced her consumption and is a moderate coffee drinker. Your father insists that she cut out all coffee and says that there is no acceptable level of coffee consumption. What does the data say about the effects of moderate caffeine use?

Critical Thinking Activity: Ethical Issues in Tobacco Advertising

Search through magazines for an example of a tobacco advertisement aimed at the following targeted groups children and teenagers, a minority group, and gender-based advertising.

Questions for the Critical Thinker

After you have completed this activity, reflect on the following questions. Your thoughtful responses will enhance your learning of this activity as well as your understanding of tobacco advertising.

1. What ethical issues are raised by advertising?

2. In your advertising search, did you find other targets of tobacco companies?

3. What appeal do the advertisements have for the targeted groups?

4. What legislative controls, if any, should be used to regulate tobacco smoke? Why or why not?

General Review Questions

Short Answer

1. What factors affect how quickly your system will absorb alcohol?

2. What are the effects of fetal alcohol syndrome?

3. Distinguish between Type 1 and Type 2 alcoholism.

4. Besides cancer, what are the health risks created by smokeless tobacco?

5. List health benefits of quitting smoking.

6. What are some of the biological effects of caffeine?

Multiple Choice

1. The process whereby yeast organisms break down plant sugars to yield ethanol is called:
   a. Fermentation
   b. Distillation
   c. Mashation
   d. Alcoholization

2. Most distilled alcoholic beverages are:
   a. 40% or higher alcohol
   b. 12% to 15% alcohol
   c. 8% to 10% alcohol
   d. 2% to 6% alcohol

3. Blood alcohol concentration (BAC) is:
   a. The concentration of plant sugars in the blood stream
   b. The percentage of alcohol in a beverage
   c. The level of alcohol content in the blood before becoming drunk
   d. The ratio of alcohol to the total blood volume

4. The majority of alcohol is absorbed into the blood stream in the:
   a. Mouth
   b. Stomach
   c. Small intestine
   d. Large intestine

5. A cardiovascular condition that results from drinking alcohol is:
   a. Cirrhosis
   b. High blood pressure
   c. Myocardial infarction
   d. Alcoholic hepatitis

6. Among women, drinking alcohol has been linked with:
   a. Vaginal cancer
   b. Ovarian cancer
   c. Uterine cancer
   d. Breast cancer

7. Fetal alcohol syndrome can cause:
   a. Mental retardation
   b. Small head
   c. Abnormalities of the face, limbs, heart, and brain
   d. All of the above

8. Approximately ___ percent of all traffic fatalities are alcohol related.
   a. 25
   b. 37
   c. 41
   d. 53

9. Margie is a junior at a prestigious university. She does not work so that she can have time for studying since her major is extremely demanding. She lives with her boyfriend, with whom she has a couple of beers on the weekend. Margie usually drinks more when they go to the local college bar, however. Why is Margie at risk for alcoholism?
   a. Because young women who attend college drink more frequently than those who do not attend college
   b. Because young women who drink and are unemployed are at increased risk for alcoholism
   c. Because young women drink and live with a partner but not are not married are at increased for alcoholism
   d. All of the above

10. Only 14 percent of women who need treatment for alcoholism get it. What is the reason(s) that more women do not get treatment?

   a. The loss of potential income prohibits some women from getting treatment

   b. The lack of child care prohibits some women from getting treatment

   c. The fear that treatment is not confidential prohibits some women from getting treatment

   d. All of the above

11. Research indicates that less than ___ percent of recovering alcoholics are able to resume drinking on a limited basis.

   a. 1

   b. 9

   c. 12

   d. 21

12. If whisky is 80 proof, what is the percentage of alcohol in the drink?

   a. 20%

   b. 40%s

   c. 60%

   d. 80%

13. A driver's BAC depends on:

   a. His or her weight and body fat

   b. The water content in his or her body tissue

   c. The volume of the alcohol

   d. All of the above

14. People who drink moderately experience which of the following effects:

   a. Shrinkage in brain size

   b. Shrinkage in brain weight

   c. A loss in some degree of intellectual ability

   d. All of the above

15. A syndrome describing children with a history of prenatal alcohol exposure but without all of the physical or behavioral symptoms of FAS is:

   a. Alcoholic Behavioral Syndrome

   b. Fetal Alcoholic Hepatitis

   c. Fetal Alcohol Effects

   d. Fetal Alcoholic Abuse

16. The thick brownish substance condensed from particulate matter in cigarette smoke is:

   a. Tar

   b. Nicotine

   c. Chewing tobacco

   d. Carbon monoxide

17. A powdered form of tobacco that is sniffed and absorbed through the mucous membranes in the nose or placed inside the cheek and sucked is called:

   a. Chewing tobacco

   b. Snuff

   c. Smoking

   d. All of the above

18. Which of the following is not a physical effect of nicotine stimulation?

   a. Constriction of blood vessels

   b. Decrease in stomach contractions

   c. Increase sensation in the taste buds

   d. Increased blood pressure

19. The leading cause of cancer death from smoking is:

   a. Throat cancer

   b. Colon cancer

   c. Lung cancer

   d. Stomach cancer

20. Stickiness of red blood cells associated with blood clots is called:

   a. Clumping

   b. Platelet adhesiveness

   c. Elevated HDLs

   d. Stroke

21. Which of the following respiratory diseases are primarily associated with smoking?
    a. Chronic bronchitis
    b. Emphysema
    c. Legionnaires disease
    d. Both a and b

22. Daily smoking of one cigar:
    a. Is a safe practice that does not increase a person's risk for health problems
    b. Increases a person's risk for cancer of the lip, tongue, mouth, larynx and lungs
    c. Is safe for others who may be exposed to the smoke
    d. Is safe because cigars do not have the harmful ingredients contained in cigarettes

23. Babies born to women who smoke during pregnancy are more likely to die from:
    a. Congenital heart failure
    b. Pneumonia
    c. Sudden infant death syndrome
    d. Infantile paralysis

24. Smoking has been associated with which of the following health effects?
    a. Gum disease
    b. Increased medication usage
    c. Impotence
    d. All of the above

25. Smoking has been shown to affect women by:
    a. Causing women to begin menopause one to two years earlier
    b. Contributing to the development of osteoporosis
    c. Increasing the risk of death from emphysema or chronic bronchitis
    d. All of the above

26. The age group with the highest percentage of smokers is:
    a. 15-24 year olds
    b. 25-44 year olds
    c. 44-55 year olds
    d. 55 year olds and older

27. The financial costs for smoking in the workplace include all of the following, except:
    a. Absenteeism
    b. Loss of productivity
    c. Training to replace employees who die prematurely
    d. Loss of time due to excessive breaks

28. Children, especially those under the age of 5, who are exposed to environmental tobacco smoke:
    a. Miss more school days
    b. Have more colds and respiratory infections
    c. Have a greater risk of pneumonia and bronchitis
    d. All of the above

29. Caffeine acts as a(n) _____ on the central nervous system.
    a. Stimulant
    b. Analgesic
    c. Depressant
    d. Hallucinogenic

30. Sensory disturbance from caffeine may be experienced after ____ cups of coffee within a 24-hour period.
    a. 3
    b. 5
    c. 7
    d. 10

Language Enrichment Glossary

In addition to the words in the Key Terms list at the end of the chapter, students listed the following words as difficult to understand. Use the chapter Key Terms list, this list, your dictionary, and teachers and friends to learn the meaning of words you do not understand.

abnormality: something wrong
absorbed: soaked in
abstinence: not do something
abysmal: extremely bad
access: reach, obtain
accumulate: gather
achieved: accomplished
acquaintance rape: forced sex by known person
adapt: adjust
addictive: creating a need
adhere: follow, stick to
adjunct: addition, supplement
adolescents: teenagers
adversely: negatively
affliction: illness, problem
agitated: disturbed, excited
airways: breathing passages
alert: warn, notify
analyzed: studied, examined
antagonizing: offending, annoying
appetite: desire to eat
aroused: stimulated
array: assortment, variety
arteries: large blood vessels
auxiliary group: group connected to a main group
aversive properties: offensive characteristics
banned: prevented, eliminated
blatant: obvious, stand out
bloodstream: blood
bombarded: attacked, overwhelmed
bowling alley: place to do bowling game
buildup: increase, gathering
bus depot: bus station
cannot stand: strongly dislike
carcinogenic: causes cancer
cardiac patient: heart patient
cardiovascular: related to heart and blood circulation
causative factor: a cause of something
cessation: stopping
characteristics: qualities

chewers:	people who chew tobacco
cigarette-induced:	caused by smoking
clogging:	blocking, plugging up
clotting:	lumps of blood
cluster:	group
coma:	long, deep unconsciousness
compensate:	to make up for
component:	part
comprehensive:	broad, includes many things
compulsive:	addicted
concentration:	amount of something present
concerted:	focused on one thing
condones:	allows, permits
confronts:	challenges
consumed:	to drink or eat
contraceptives:	birth control
contractions:	squeezing
converted:	changed
correlated:	associated
counselling:	talking treatment
cravings:	desires for something
cure:	remedy to heal a disease
decaffeinated:	caffeine taken out
decisive:	definite, determining
delusions:	false perceptions
deformities:	unhealthy development
denying:	preventing
dependent on:	need or rely on something
depicted:	shown
depleted:	lowered
deprivation:	shortage
derive:	gain, obtain from
designate:	choose
despite:	in spite of
dilute:	weaken
diminish:	make smaller
dippers:	people who suck tobacco, use chewing tobacco
disputed:	argued about
distribution:	to deliver, spread
dominated:	controlled
doomed:	expected bad outcome
dosage:	amount
dramatically:	significantly
drinking spree:	overindulgence in drinking
dump:	toss out, unload

dysfunction:	not working correctly
elegant:	cultured, luxurious
emulating:	imitating
enacted:	made
endured:	suffered, tolerated
enhance:	increase
entails:	involves
entice:	tempt
eradicate:	eliminate, get rid of
err on the side of:	make a cautious, conservative choice
euphoric:	feeling of great happiness
exacerbate:	make worse
exert:	creates
exhale:	breathe out
exhausted:	very tired
expelled:	sent out
extended family:	relatives beyond immediate family
extremely:	very
fast food:	already prepared food
fatigue:	tiredness
fetuses:	unborn babies not completely formed
fibrous:	resembling fibres twisted together
flawed:	containing mistakes
gauging:	measuring
graduate:	to move on to
harmless:	doesn't damage
hazardous:	dangerous
heartbeat:	pulses of the heart
heartburn:	stomach indigestion
higher power:	spiritual belief in something greater than humans
impairs:	limits
impinge upon:	influence negatively
inalienable right:	undeniable, absolute right
inconclusive:	indefinite, undetermined
in conjunction with:	happens at the same time
in contrast:	in comparison
indication:	measure, a sign of
inebriated:	drunk
ingest:	drink or eat
inhibit:	slow down, restrict
inhibitions:	personal reservations
insomnia:	inability to sleep
instituting:	establishing
interfere:	interrupt, obstruct
intoxicated:	drunk

irritate:	bother, inflame
jawbone:	bone in bottom of face
judiciously:	choose carefully
lag:	delay
letdown:	tired, sad feeling
liqueurs:	sweet, condensed alcoholic drinks
localized:	staying in a specific area
long-term:	done for a long time
loosen up:	relax
mental functioning:	brain activity
metabolized:	chemical process of being absorbed into and used by the body
miscarriage:	too early delivery of a fetus
moderate:	medium
molasses:	brown sugar syrup
momentum:	increased acceptance
monitor:	watch, supervise
motor impairment:	muscle handicap
nicotine:	addictive chemical in tobacco
nonusers:	those who don't use
noxious:	unpleasant, repulsive
obesity:	overweight, fat
on occasion:	once in a while
opponents:	those who disagree
optional complement:	voluntary addition
overrepresented:	more than expected
paralysis:	inability to move
paralyzing:	causing to not move
peers:	people of similar age, status
per capita:	per person
persuaded:	convinced, influence
pleasant lift:	good feeling
plug:	large piece of tobacco
pollutant:	something which makes air or water harmful
primarily:	mainly, basically
prioritized:	placed in order of importance
prolonged:	continued, extended
psychoactive:	chemicals which affect mental states
puff:	breath of smoke
quid:	thick piece
quitters:	people who stop something
rapidly:	very fast, quickly
readily:	easily, quickly
receding:	pulling back
receptor:	nerve ending which receives a stimulus
recommended:	suggested as a good idea

recreational drug:	drugs taken for pleasure
refrain:	avoid doing something
refuting:	disagreeing with
resiliency:	ability to bounce back from problems
resolve:	decide, commit
respiratory rate:	rate of breathing
retards:	slows
revocation:	cancellation
roommate:	person who shares a living space
saliva:	moisture in the mouth
sensitive:	easily affected
setting:	surrounding situation
shrinkage:	contraction, becoming smaller
severe:	strong
smoker's breath:	bad breath caused by smoking
sobering:	serious, solemn
social living group:	people in one's daily life
solution:	mixture
sophisticated:	refined, worldly
spouse battering:	physical abuse of spouse
staggering:	shocking, overwhelming
steadfastly:	unfailingly
stigma:	social disgrace, shame
substantial:	large
sudden:	unexpected, quick
suffocate:	die from lack of air in lungs
synaptic junctions:	points of nerve connections
theoretically:	assumed
tobacco industry:	companies which make, sell tobacco
tolerance to:	resistance to
transported:	carried
urbanization:	becoming like a city
value-related:	connected with morals and beliefs
variable:	various, changeable
vessels:	blood veins
vital functions:	temperature, pulse and breathing rate
vulnerable:	sensitive to something
weaken:	make weak
weaned:	to give up a habit
wheezing:	difficult, noisy breathing
withdrawal symptoms:	bad feelings from stopping something

CHAPTER 12
Cardiovascular Disease and Cancer: Reducing Your Risks

Chapter Overview

Cardiovascular disease (CVDs) are the leading cause of death in Canada today, accounting for more than 37 percent of all deaths. Despite this statistic, a number of factors have contributed to increasing optimism about treating and preventing CVD, including advances in medical techniques, earlier and better diagnostic procedures and treatments, improved emergency medical assistance programs, and training of ordinary citizens in cardiopulmonary resuscitation (CPR). It is important to know how the cardiovascular system functions. The cardiovascular system is the network of elastic tubes through which blood flows as it carries oxygen and nutrients to ail parts of the body. For the heart to function properly, the four chambers must beat in an organized manner. The average adult heart at rest beats 70 to 80 times per minute. When overly stressed, a heart may beat over 200 times per minute, especially in an individual who is overweight or out of shape. A healthy heart functions more efficiently and is less likely to suffer damage from overwork than is an unhealthy one.

The most common forms of heart disease include atherosclerosis, heart attack, chest pain, irregular heartbeat, congestive heart failure, congenital and rheumatic heart disease, and stroke.

Risk factors for cardiovascular disease are divided into two types those that can be controlled and those that cannot. Risks you can control include cigarette smoking, high blood fat and cholesterol levels, hypertension, lack of exercise, high-fat diet, obesity, diabetes, and emotional stress. Risks you cannot control include heredity, age, gender, and race.

While men do have more heart attacks and have them earlier in life, women have a much lower chance of surviving a heart attack. Premenopausal women are unlikely candidates for heart attacks, except for those who suffer from diabetes, high blood pressure, kidney disease, or who have a genetic predisposition to high cholesterol levels. Family history and smoking can also increase the risk for premenopausal women. Once her estrogen production drops with menopause, a woman's chances of developing CVD rise rapidly. Symptoms of heart disease in postmenopausal women often are manifested differently than in men. Research suggests three main reasons for widespread neglect of the signs of heart disease in women physicians may be gender-biased, physicians tend to view male heart disease as a more severe problem, and women decline major procedures more often than do men.

Several methods are used to diagnose heart disease, including electrocardiogram, angiography, and positron emission tomography scans. New methods developed for treating heart blockages include radionuclide imaging, magnetic resonance imaging, and digital cardiac angiography. During the 1980s, coronary bypass surgery seemed to be the ultimate method for treating patients who had coronary blockages or who had suffered heart attacks. Recently, experts have begun to question the effectiveness of bypass operations, particularly for elderly people. A procedure called angioplasty is associated with fewer risks and is believed by many experts to be more effective than bypass surgery in selected cardiovascular cases. Research has indicated that the use of low-dose aspirin is beneficial to heart patients. However, gastrointestinal intolerance is a major problem associated with aspirin use, and this factor may outweigh its benefits for some people. If a heart attack occurs, and a victim gets to an emergency room fast enough, a form of reperfusion therapy called thrombolysis can sometimes be performed.

Cancer is the name given to a large group of diseases characterized by the uncontrolled growth and spread of abnormal cells. These cells may create tumours. Cancerous tumours are called malignant, while noncancerous tumours, the majority of tumours, are benign. A biopsy determines whether a given tumour or mass is benign or malignant.

Scientists have proposed several theories for the cellular changes that produce cancer, including spontaneous error, environmental carcinogens, and oncogenes. Some of the most widely suspected causes of cancer include biological factors, occupational/environmental factors, social and psychological factors, food chemicals, viral factors, medical factors, and combinations of these factors.

There are four broad classifications of cancer, depending upon the type of tissue from which the cancer arises. Carcinomas are in the epithelial tissues; sarcomas occur in the mesodermal, or middle, layers of tissue; lymphomas develop in the lymphatic system; and leukaemia is cancer of the blood-forming parts of the body, particularly the bone marrow and spleen. Common cancers include lung, breast, colon and rectum, prostate, skin, testicular, ovarian, uterine, pancreas, leukaemia, and oral cancers.

The earlier a person is diagnosed as having cancer, the better the prospect for survival. Various high-tech diagnostic techniques exist to detect cancer. These medical techniques, along with regular self-examinations and checkups, play an important role in the early detection and secondary prevention of cancer. Although cancer treatments have changed significantly over the last 20 years, surgery, in which the tumour and surrounding tissue are removed, is still common. Today's surgeons tend to remove less surrounding tissue than they did previously, and to combine surgery with either radiotherapy or chemotherapy to kill cancerous cells. There are many other promising advances in the cancer treatments, including the use of tamoxifen, immunotherapy, magnetic resonance imaging, a powerful enzyme inhibitor called TIMP-2, a metastasis suppresser gene called NM23, neoadjuvant chemotherapy, and prostatic ultrasound.

Learning Objectives

1. Describe the anatomy and physiology of the heart and the circulatory system.
2. Review the various types of heart disease and their diagnoses and treatments.
3. Identify the controllable risk factors for cardiovascular disease. Examine the risk factors you cannot control.
4. Discuss the issues uniquely concerning women in relationship to cardiovascular disease.
5. Discuss some of the new methods of diagnosis and treatment of cardiovascular disease.
6. Define cancer and discuss how cancer develops.
7. Discuss the probable causes of cancer, including biological causes, occupational and environmental causes, social and psychological causes, chemicals in foods, viral causes, medical causes, and combined causes.
8. Understand and act in response to self-exams, medical exams, and symptoms related to different types of cancer.
9. Discuss cancer detection and treatment, including radiation therapy, chemotherapy, and immunotherapy.

Key Terms

Fill in a brief definition to help you remember these terms.

cardiovascular disease (CVDs) _____

cardiovascular system _____

atria _____

ventricles _____

arteries _____

arterioles _____

capillaries _____

veins _____

sinoatrial node (SA node) _____

atherosclerosis _____

plaque _____

myocardial infarction (MI) _____

heart attack _____

coronary thrombosis _____

collateral circulation _____

ischemia _____

angina pectoris _____

beta blockers _____

arrhythmia _____

fibrillation _____

congenital heart disease _____

rheumatic heart disease _____

stroke _____

thrombus _____

embolus _____

aneurysm _____

transient ischemic attacks (TIAs) _____

low-density lipoproteins (LDLs) _____

high-density lipoproteins (HDLs) _____

triglycerides _____

hypertension _____

essential hypertension _____

secondary hypertension _____

systolic pressure _____

diastolic pressure _____

hormone replacement therapies (HRT) _____

electrocardiogram (ECG) _____

angiography _____

positron emission tomography (PET scan) _____

coronary bypass surgery _____

angioplasty _____

thrombolysis _____

cancer _____

neoplasm _____

tumour _____

malignant _____

benign _____

biopsy _____

metastasis _____

mutant cells _____

carcinogens _____

oncogenes _____

protooncogenes _____

oncologists_____

malignant melanoma _____

PAP test _____

radiotherapy_____

chemotherapy _____

immunotherapy _____

magnetic resonance imaging (MRI) _____

computerized axial tomography (CAT scan)_____

prostate-specific antigen (PSA) _____

Critical Thinking Exercises

1. Summarize ways to reduce risks for heart attack. Identify those that may apply to you.

2. Noreen just experienced menopause. Her doctor explained that once her estrogen production drops with menopause, her chances of developing CVD rise rapidly. Explain the role of estrogen as a risk factor for heart disease.

3. Sandy believes that it is her responsibility for cancer detection. What seven warning signals is she aware of?

4. Fifty-two-year-old Stan and 50-year-old Susan believe in taking responsibility for their health. They want to make sure that appropriate diagnostic tests for cancer are done. What tests should each have and how often should these tests be done?

Critical Thinking Activity: Reviewing Personal Risk Factors for Cancer

Describe six aspects of your life that tend to increase your risk for developing cancer, for example, smoking. Identify why you engage in these high-risk behaviours, indicate whether you plan to change these behaviours, and list any measures you plan to take which could lower these risks.

General Review Questions

Short Answer

1. Name the common forms of cardiovascular disease.

2. Distinguish between tachycardia and bradycardia.

3. List reasons for neglect of heart disease symptoms in women.

4. How do benign and malignant tumours differ?

5. Name the four classifications of cancer.

6. What are warning signals of breast cancer? What are the risk factors for breast cancer?

7. What are symptoms of prostate cancer?

8. What is the most common risk factor for oral cancer?

Multiple Choice

1 . The leading cause of death in Canada is:
   a. Strokes
   b. Transient Ischemic Attacks
   c. Cardiovascular Diseases
   d. Cancer

2. The part of the cardiovascular system that takes blood away from the heart is(are) the:
   a. Atrium
   b. Veins
   c. Capillaries
   d. Arteries

3. A blockage of the normal blood supply to an area of the heart is called:
   a. A stroke
   b. A coronary thrombosis
   c. A heart attack
   d. Angina pectoris

4. An irregularity in heartbeat is called:
   a. Fibrillation
   b. Bradycardia
   c. Tachycardia
   d. Arrhythmia

5. The drug used to dilate veins and reduce the amount of blood returning to the heart and thus lessening its workload is:
   a. Nitroglycerin
   b. Inderal
   c. Prinivil
   d. Lopressor

6. When the blood supply to the brain is cut off, the result may be:
   a. A myocardial infarction
   b. A thrombosis
   c. A stroke
   d. An aneurysm

7. Nonessential hypertension is caused by:
   a. Smoking
   b. Obesity
   c. Kidney disease
   d. No specific cause

8. A surgical technique whereby a blood vessel is implanted to bypass a blocked artery is called:
   a. Angioplasty
   b. Coronary by-pass surgery
   c. Electrocardiogram
   d. Pacemaker implantation

9. The organ that is a muscular, four-chambered pump that is roughly the size of a man's fist is:
   a. The heart
   b. The capillaries
   c. The lungs
   d. The atria

10. The mitral valve is located:
    a. Between the right ventricle and the pulmonary artery
    b. Between the left atrium and the left ventricle
    c. Between the right atrium and the right ventricle
    d. Between the left ventricle and the aorta

11. An abnormally fast heartbeat is known as:
    a. Arrhythmia
    b. Tachycardia
    c. Vasodilation
    d. Aneurysm

12. What are the underlying causes of congenital heart disease?
    a. Maternal diseases
    b. Chemical intake by the mother during pregnancy
    c. Streptococcal infection
    d. All of the above

13. Which of the following is(are) the symptom(s) of a transient ischemic attack?
    a. Sudden weakness or numbness of the face, arm, or leg on one side of the body
    b. Loss of speech, or trouble talking or understanding speech
    c. Sudden, severe headaches with no known cause
    d. All of the above

14. The variety of cholesterol that is associated with cardiovascular risks is:
    a. High-density lipoproteins
    b. Very high-density lipoproteins
    c. Low-density lipoproteins
    d. Omega-3 transfatty acids

15. The diagnostic technique that uses powerful magnets to look inside the body is called:
    a. Radionuclide imaging
    b. Magnetic resonance imaging
    c. Digital cardiac angiography
    d. Cardiomagnetic angioplasty

16. The development of new, small blood vessels that reroute needed blood through other areas as a result of minor heart blockage is called:
    a. Coronary circulation
    b. Collateral circulation
    c. Converse circulation
    d. Coronary thrombosis

17. Severe chest pain occurring as a result of reduced oxygen flow to the heart is called:
    a. Angina pectoris
    b. Arrhythmias
    c. Myocardial infarction
    d. Congestive heart failure

18. A type of heart disease caused by untreated streptococcal infection of the throat is:
    a. Congestive heart failure
    b. Congenital heart disease
    c. Rheumatic heart disease
    d. Coronary thrombosis

19. When a neoplasmic mass forms a clumping of cells it is called:
    a. Cancer
    b. Neoplasm
    c. A tumor
    d. Carcinogen

20. Which of the following is a source (are sources) of ionizing radiation?
    a. Radon
    b. Microwaves
    c. Computer screens
    d. Electric blankets

21. Human Papilloma virus has been linked to:
   a. Testicular cancer
   b. Breast cancer
   c. Cervical cancer
   d. Ovarian cancer

22. Cancer of the blood-forming parts of the body, particularly the bone marrow and spleen, is called:
   a. Lymphoma
   b. Leukemia
   c. Carcinoma
   d. Sarcoma

23. The second leading cause of cancer death in males is:
   a. Lung cancer
   b. Breast cancer
   c. Testicular cancer
   d. Prostate cancer

24. The treatment of skin cancer that involves tissue destruction by freezing is called:
   a. Surgery
   b. Cryosurgery
   c. Electrodesication
   d. Radiation therapy

25. Cancers that occur in the mesodermal layers of tissue (i.e., bones, muscles, and general connective tissues) are called:
   a. Carcinomas
   b. Lymphomas
   c. Leukemia
   d. Sarcomas

26. A yearly Pap test and pelvic exam should be performed if:
   a. A woman is sexually active
   b. A woman is over the age of 18
   c. Only if a woman has a history of cervical cancer
   d. Both a and b

27. A large group of diseases characterized by uncontrolled growth and spread of abnormal cells is called:
   a. Mutant cells
   b. Neoplasms
   c. Carcinogens
   d. Cancer

28. The most common and most dangerous carcinogen is:
   a. Coal tar
   b. Tar in cigarettes
   c. Radiation
   d. Pesticides

29. Physicians who specialize in the treatment of malignancies are called:
   a. Oncologists
   b. Internalists
   c. Cancerologists
   d. Epidemiologists

30. Risk factors for breast cancer include all of the following, except:
   a. Female, under the age of 20
   b. Family history, in particular a grandmother, mother, or sister
   c. Female, never had children
   d. Female, first child after the age of 30

Language Enrichment Glossary

In addition to the words in the Key Terms list at the end of the chapter, students listed the following words as difficult to understand. Use the chapter Key Terms list, this list, your dictionary, and teachers and friends to learn the meaning of words you do not understand.

abnormalities:	unexpected outcomes
acute:	severe
agent:	cause
aggressive:	done with intensity, commitment
at risk:	likely to get
avid:	eager
benign:	not harmful
blood-streaked:	marked with blood
causal link:	connection between cause and effect
chronic:	periodic, long-lasting
circumvent:	get around
clusters:	groups
comply with:	agree to
compounded:	increased
conflicting data:	differing information
counterparts:	similar people
curtailed:	limited, ended
demographically similar:	similar characteristics
diuretics:	substances that increase urination
emits:	to put out
enhance:	increase
epidemiological:	studies of epidemic diseases
fashion:	way
gender-biased:	influenced by beliefs about one gender
given:	specific
governed:	regulated, supervised
grad:	graduate
hazards:	dangers
hemorrhaging:	bleeding which doesn't stop
imaging:	procedures for looking at something
imperative:	necessary
insure:	guarantee
internalize:	keep inside
intolerance:	negative reaction, inability to tolerate
invasive:	intruding
likelihood:	probability
lobbied:	pushed for
longitudinal study:	study comparing information at different times
mammogram:	breast x-ray
manifestation:	evidence, symptom

monitoring:	watching, checking
opportunistic:	taking advantage of a situation
optimism:	cheerfulness, positive outlook
options:	choices
oral cavity:	mouth and upper throat
orthodox:	traditional
overwhelmed:	surprised, overcome
pacemaker:	mechanism that regulates heartbeats
particular:	specific
pigmented:	colore
pose:	present, cause
programmed:	set
prolonged:	extended over a long time
prone:	a tendency toward
proposes:	suggests
quivering:	shaking, trembling
readily:	easily
routinely:	usually
sedentary:	inactive
shove… in your face:	place something abruptly in front of you
site:	location
skeptical:	not believing
spasm:	muscle contraction, seizure
sporadic:	periodic, irregular
sputum:	mucus coughed up from the lungs
suspect:	suspicious
tampering:	adjusting, changing
taxed:	overworked, strained
therapeutic:	treatment of an illness
underway:	occurring
unique challenge:	specific difficulty
variability:	variation
virulent:	disease which spreads rapidly
warranted:	justified, called for

CHAPTER 13
Infectious and Noninfectious Conditions: Risks and Responsibilities

Chapter Overview

Most diseases are multifactorial. For a disease to occur, the host must be susceptible, an agent capable of transmitting a disease must be present, and the environment must be hospitable to the pathogen. Other risk factors also apparently increase or decrease levels of susceptibility. Some of the most common uncontrollable risk factors are heredity, aging, and environmental conditions. Controllable risk factors include too much stress, inadequate nutrition, a low physical fitness level, lack of sleep, misuse or abuse of legal and illegal substances, personal hygiene, and high-risk behaviours.

There are numerous ways that pathogens enter the body: direct contact, such as during sexual relations; indirect contact, such as by touching an object the infected person has had contact with; autoinoculation; airborne contact; food-borne infection; animal-borne pathogens; and water-borne diseases. The most common pathogens are bacteria, viruses, fungi, protozoa, and parasitic worms.

Body defenses include physical and chemical defenses, the immune system, fever, pain, vaccines, and active and passive immunity.

There are over 20 different types of sexually transmitted infections (STIs). A stigma associated with these diseases often keeps infected people from seeking treatment, and these people usually continue to be sexually active, thereby infecting unsuspecting partners. People who are uncomfortable discussing sexual issues may also be less likely to use and/or ask their partners to use condoms as a means of protecting against STIs and/or pregnancy. Also, the casual attitude about sex that prevails today lends itself to not considering the consequences. In addition, many STIs are asymptomatic in some people and the infected person may unknowingly spread the disease to an unsuspecting partner. Sexually transmitted infections are generally spread through some form of intimate sexual contact. Sexual intercourse, oral-genital contact, hand-genital contact, and anal intercourse are the most common modes of transmission. Chlamydia is the most common STI among heterosexuals. Unfortunately, many chlamydia victims display no symptoms and therefore do not seek help until the disease has done secondary damage, which is serious in both sexes. Chlamydia can be controlled through responsible sexual behaviour and familiarity with the early symptoms of the disease. If detected early enough, chlamydia is easily treatable with antibiotics. Pelvic inflammatory disease refers to a number of infections of the uterus, fallopian tubes, and ovaries. PID is often the result of an untreated sexually transmitted disease, but nonsexual causes of PID are also common, such as excessive vaginal douching or cigarette smoking. Gonorrhea primarily infects the linings of the urethra, genital tract, pharynx, and rectum. It may be spread to the eyes or other body regions via the hands or body fluids. If syphilis is left untreated, the disease progresses from the primary stage to the secondary, latent, and late stages, with devastating consequences. Treatment for syphilis is with antibiotics. The major obstacle to treatment is misdiagnosis of this "imitator" disease. Pubic lice are small parasites that are usually transmitted during sexual contact. Venereal warts are caused by human papilloma viruses (HPVs). A person becomes infected when an HPV penetrates the skin and mucous membranes of the genitals or anus through sexual contact. Candidiasis is a yeast-like fungus caused by the candida albicans organism that normally inhabits the vaginal tract in most women. Only under certain conditions will these organisms multiply to abnormal quantities and begin to cause problems. Trichomoniasis is caused by a protozoan. Although usually transmitted by sexual contact, the "trich" organism may be easily spread by toilet seats, wet towels, or other items that have discharged fluids on them. Some forms of general urinary tract infections are sexually transmitted. Herpes is a general term for a family of diseases characterized by sores or eruptions on the skin. Herpes simplex virus type 1 causes cold sores and fever blisters. Genital herpes is caused by herpes simplex virus type 2.

Acquired immune deficiency syndrome (AIDS) is a major health problem in the world today. Death rates continue to escalate, and no cure has been found. AIDS is caused by the human immunodeficiency virus (HIV). HIV is not an infection that affects certain groups because of inherent group characteristics, but rather, an equal-opportunity pathogen that can attack anyone who engages in certain high-risk behaviours. The HIV virus typically enters one person's body when another person's infected body fluids gain entry through a breach in body defenses. Mucous membranes of the genital organs and the anus provide the easiest route of entry. High-risk activities that are known to spread the virus include exchange of body fluids, receiving a blood transfusion prior to 1986, injection drug users, and mother-to-infant transmission (perinatal). A person may go for months or years after infection by HIV before any significant symptoms appear. The incubation times varies greatly from person to person. Children have shorter incubation periods than do adults. The ELISA and Western blot tests detect antibodies of the disease, indicating the presence of the HIV in the person's system. Although the list of possible anti-HIV agents has grown considerably in the last five years, many would-be cures remain on the unapproved list for human testing. Of those that have gained approval, zidovudine (AZT) has had promising results. The only effective prevention strategies known all closely relate to the means by which people contract AIDS. You can reduce your risks by the choices you make in sexual behaviours and the responsibilities you take for your health and for that of your loved ones.

Noninfectious and chronic diseases are not transmitted by any pathogen or by any form of personal contact. They usually develop over a long length of time, and they cause progressive damage to human tissues. Lifestyle and personal health habits appear to be major contributing factors to the general rise in the incidence of chronic diseases in recent years.

Allergies are a result of the body's attempt to defend itself against a specific antigen or allergen by producing specific antibodies. Respiratory disorders include hay fever, asthma, emphysema, and chronic bronchitis. Hay fever attacks are characterized by sneezing and itchy, watery eyes and nose. Asthma is characterized by attacks of wheezing, difficulty in breathing, shortness of breath, and coughing spasms. Emphysema involves the gradual destruction of the alveoli of the lungs. As the alveoli are destroyed, the affected person finds it more and more difficult to exhale. In chronic bronchitis, the bronchial tubes become so inflamed and swollen that normal respiratory function is impaired. Symptoms of chronic bronchitis include a productive cough and shortness of breath that persists for several weeks.

Headaches may result from dilated blood vessels within the brain, underlying organic problems, or excessive stress and anxiety. The most common forms of headaches are tension, migraine, secondary, and psychological headaches. There are several forms of seizure disorders, including grand mal, petit mal, psychomotor, and Jacksonian seizures.

Common female disorders include fibrocystic breast condition, premenstrual syndrome, and endometriosis. Fibrocystic breast condition is a common noncancerous problem among women. Symptoms range in severity from a small palpable lump to large masses of irregular tissue found in both breasts. Premenstrual syndrome is characterized by depression, tension, irritability, headaches, tender breasts, bloated abdomen, backache, abdominal cramps, acne, fluid retention, diarrhea, and fatigue. Endometriosis is characterized by the abnormal growth and development of endometrial tissue in regions of the body other than the uterus. Symptoms include severe cramping during and between menstrual cycles, irregular periods, unusually heavy or light menstrual flow, abdominal bloating, fatigue, painful bowel movements with periods, painful intercourse, constipation, diarrhea, menstrual pain, infertility, and low back pain.

Diabetes occurs when the pancreas fails to produce enough insulin to regulate sugar metabolism or when the body fails to use insulin effectively. Diabetics exhibit hyperglycemia and high glucose levels in their urine. Other symptoms include excessive thirst, frequent urination, hunger, tendency to tire easily, wounds that heal slowly, numbness or tingling in the extremities, changes in vision, skin eruptions, and, in women, a tendency toward vaginal yeast infections. Colitis is a disease of the large intestine in which the mucous membranes of the intestinal walls become inflamed. Symptoms include bloody diarrhea, severe stomach cramps, weight loss, nausea, sweating, and fever. Related to colitis is irritable bowel syndrome which is characterized by nausea, pain, gas, diarrhea attacks, or cramps after eating specific foods or when a person is under unusual stress. Diverticulosis occurs when the walls of the intestine become weakened for unknown reasons and small pea-sized bulges develop. These bulges often fill with feces and, over time, become irritated and infected. If this irritation persists, bleeding and chronic obstruction may occur, either of which can be life-threatening. Peptic ulcers occur when stomach acids irritate the stomach or intestinal lining. It is caused by the erosive effect of digestive juices on these tissues. Gallbladder disease is a result of the gallbladder being repeatedly irritated by chemicals, infection, or overuse, thus reducing its ability to release bile used for the digestion of fats. One of the characteristic symptoms of gallbladder disease is acute pain in the upper right portion of the abdomen after eating fatty foods.

Musculoskeletal diseases include arthritis, systemic lupus erythematosus (SLE), scleroderma, Raynaud's syndrome, and low back pain. Symptoms of arthritis range from the occasional tendinitis of the weekend athlete to the terrible pain of rheumatoid arthritis. Osteoarthritis is a progressive deterioration of bones and joints. Rheumatoid arthritis is an inflammatory joint disease. Symptoms may be gradually progressive or sporadic, with occasional unexplained remissions. Rheumatoid arthritis typically attacks the synovial membrane, which produces the lubricating fluids for the joints. Advanced rheumatoid arthritis often involves destruction of the bony ends of joints. Lupus is a disease in which the immune system attacks the body, producing antibodies that destroy or injure organs such as the kidneys, brain, and heart. The symptoms vary from mild to severe and may disappear for periods of time. A butterfly-shaped rash covering the bridge of the nose and both cheeks is common. Nearly all SLE sufferers have aching joints and muscles, and many develop redness and swelling that moves from joint to joint. Low back pain (LBP) episodes may result from muscular damage and be short-lived and acute, or may involve dislocations, fractures, or other problems with spinal vertebrae or discs and be chronic or require surgery.

The diagnosis of chronic fatigue syndrome depends on two major criteria and eight or more minor criteria. The major criteria are debilitating fatigue that persists for at least six months and the absence of diagnoses of other illnesses that could cause the symptoms. Minor criteria include headaches, fever, sore throat, painful lymph nodes, weakness, fatigue after exercise, sleep problems, and rapid onset of these symptoms. Carpal tunnel syndrome is a common occupational injury in which the median nerve in the wrist becomes irritated, creating numbness, tingling, and pain in the fingers and hands. This condition is worsened by the repetitive typing motions made by computer users.

Learning Objectives

1. Discuss the risk factors for infectious diseases, including those you can control and those you cannot.
2. Describe the most common pathogens.

3. Discuss the immune system and explain the role of vaccinations in fighting disease.

4. Discuss the various sexually transmitted diseases, their means of transmission, and actions that prevent the spread of STIs.

5. Discuss the transmission, symptoms, treatment, and prevention of transmission of the HIV virus.

6. Identify common respiratory disorders.

7. Explain the common neurological disorders, including the varied types of headaches and seizure disorders.

8. Describe the common gender disorders, risk factors for these conditions, their symptoms, prevention, and control.

9. Discuss diseases of the digestive system, including their symptoms, prevention, and control.

10. Discuss the varied musculoskeletal diseases and their effects on the body.

Key Terms

Fill in a brief definition to help you remember these terms.

pathogen _____

epidemic _____

virulent _____

multifactorial disease _____

sickle-cell anemia _____

immunological competence _____

autoinoculation _____

bacteria _____

toxins _____

staphylococci _____

epidermis _____

toxic shock syndrome _____

streptococci _____

pneumonia _____

penicillin _____

tuberculosis (TB)_____

periodontal diseases _____

rickettsia _____

viruses _____

incubation period_____

slow-acting viruses _____

interferon_____

endemic_____

influenza _____

hepatitis_____

measles _____

German measles (rubella) _____

rabies_____

asymptomatic _____

fungi _____

protozoa_____

enzymes_____

antigen_____

antibodies _____

vaccination _____

sexually transmitted infections (STIs)_____

chlamydia _____

conjunctivitis_____

pelvic inflammatory disease (PID) _____

gonorrhea _____

syphilis _____

chancre _____

pubic lice _____

venereal warts _____

candidiasis _____

vaginitis _____

trichomoniasis _____

genital herpes _____

acquired immune deficiency syndrome (AIDS) _____

human immunodeficiency virus (HIV) _____

ELISA _____

western blot _____

allergy _____

histamines _____

hay fever _____

asthma _____

emphysema _____

alveoli _____

chronic bronchitis _____

migraine _____

epilepsy _____

fibrocystic breast condition _____

premenstrual syndrome (PMS) _____

endometriosis _____

hysterectomy _____

insulin _____

diabetes _____

hyperglycemia _____

ulcerative colitis _____

irritable bowel syndrome (IBS)_____

diverticulosis_____

peptic ulcer _____

arthritis _____

osteoarthritis _____

rheumatoid arthritis_____

lupus _____

Critical Thinking Exercises

1.   List five controllable risk factors for infectious diseases. Which of these factors put you at risk? What do you need to change to lessen your risk for disease?

2.   Janet is taking her newborn to the pediatrician. She is concerned about her baby receiving any vaccines because she doesn't understand how they work. How do vaccinations work? What vaccines are recommended in childhood?

3.   If you choose to be sexually active, the most effective agent for reducing the risk of STI infection to date is the condom. What can you do to protect yourself from STIs with the use of condoms?

4.   Joyce has a new boyfriend. She is uncomfortable about discussing practicing safe sex with him, because she doesn't want him to think that she doesn't trust him. What one-on-one communication skills would help Joyce address her concerns with her boyfriend?

5.   Gary has been diagnosed with a peptic ulcer. What should he avoid so that his condition is not exacerbated?

6.   Olivia is a typist for a publishing company. She was recently diagnosed with carpal tunnel syndrome. Describe her condition, and discuss how she can alleviate her suffering.

Critical Thinking Activity: Campaigning Against Risky Behaviours

It is not the mere fact of membership in a so-called high-risk group (for example, homosexuals, prostitutes, or intravenous drug users) that increases the probability of HIV infection, rather, it is the risky behaviours. What campaign effort could be mounted to effectively convey this message to the general public? Outline your ideas.

General Review Questions

Short Answer

1. List three routes of invasion for pathogens and provide an example of each.
2. What is an example of an autoimmune disease?
3. Distinguish between acquired and natural immunity.
4. List reasons for the high rates of sexually transmitted infections (STIs).
5. Identify high-risk behaviours for contracting AIDS.
6. What is the greatest risk for epileptics whose seizures are uncontrolled?
7. What is fibrocystic breast condition?
8. Describe systemic lupus erythematosus.

Multiple Choice

1. Touching the handle of a towel dispenser that has just been touched by a person whose hands were contaminated by a sneeze is an example of:
   a. Direct contact
   b. Indirect contact
   c. Food-borne transmission
   d. Airborne transmission

2. Microorganisms that are disease-causing agents are called:
   a. Endogenous microorganisms
   b. Virulent organisms
   c. Pathogens
   d. All of the above

3. Which of the following is a (are) controllable risk factor(s) for infectious diseases?
   a. Too much stress
   b. Inadequate diet
   c. Lack of sleep
   d. All of the above

4. Which of the following is(are) a major type of bacteria?
   a. Cocci
   b. Bacilli
   c. Spirilla
   d. All of the above

5. The time between when an agent breaks through the body's defenses and the first appearance of symptoms is called the:
   a. Infection period
   b. Incubation period
   c. Antibody period
   d. Immune period

6. A viral disease that causes inflammation of the liver is:
   a. Hepatitis
   b. Herpes simplex
   c. AIDS
   d. Measles

7. Single-celled organisms that cause diseases such as trichomoniasis and giardiasis are called:
   a. Fungi
   b. Bacteria
   c. Rickettsia
   d. Protozoa

8. Which of the following infections is caused by fungi?
   a. Ringworm
   b. Trichomoniasis
   c. Rabies
   d. Pneumonia

9. Treatments that are administered orally or by injection for the purpose of forming an artificial immunity are called:
   a. Vaccinations
   b. Acquired immunity
   c. Natural immunity
   d. Passive immunity

10. The most common mode of transmission for sexually transmitted infections is(are):
    a. Sexual intercourse
    b. Hand-genital contact
    c. Oral-genital contact
    d. All of the above

11. The stage of syphilis that is often characterized by the development of a sore known as a chancre is:
    a. Primary syphilis
    b. Secondary syphilis
    c. Latent syphilis
    d. Late syphilis

12. Human papilloma viruses have been associated with increased risk of:
    a. Chancres
    b. Blistering sores or eruptions on the skin
    c. Cervical cancer
    d. Pelvic inflammatory disease

13. In adults, the average length of time it takes HIV to cause slow, degenerative changes in the immune system is:
    a. 4-6 years
    b. 8-10 years
    c. 11-13 years
    d. 15 years or longer

14. The blood test used to detect the presence of HIV antibodies is the:
    a. ELISA
    b. HIV antibody test
    c. HIV-1 immunoassay
    d. Colposcopy

15. One of the most widespread sexually transmitted infections in the world is:
    a. HIV infection
    b. Genital herpes
    c. Genital warts
    d. Trichomoniasis

16. A respiratory disease in which the alveoli of the lungs are gradually destroyed is known as:
    a. Asthma
    b. Hay fever
    c. Emphysema
    d. Chronic Bronchitis

17. Epilepsy is:
    a. Localized headaches on only one side of the head
    b. A neurological disorder caused by abnormal electrical brain activity
    c. Characterized by excruciating pain that lasts for minutes or hours
    d. A hereditary disease that is more common in women than men

18. Migraine headaches are characterized by all of the following except:
    a. Primarily treated with relaxation training and biofeedback
    b. Are more common among women than men
    c. Occur when blood vessels in the membrane that surrounds the brain dilate
    d. Often are accompanied by nausea and sensitivity to light and sounds

19. Symptoms for diabetes include all of the following except:
    a. Excessive thirst
    b. Hypoglycemia
    c. Frequent urination
    d. Skin eruptions

20. Type-2 Diabetes is:
    a. Adult-onset diabetes
    b. Non-insulin dependent
    c. Tends to develop later in life
    d. All of the above

21. When the gallbladder has been repeatedly irritated and reduces its ability to release bile, a disease that can result is:
    a. Diverticulosis
    b. Colitis
    c. Cholecystitis
    d. Appendicitis

22. Rheumatoid arthritis is:
    a. A progressive deterioration of the bones and joints
    b. Affected by weather changes, excessive strain and injury
    c. An autoimmune disorder that attacks the synovial membrane which produces the lubricating fluids of the joint
    d. Caused by abnormal use of the joint and abnormalities in joint structure

23. The risk of low back pain can be reduced by all of the following except:
    a. Exercises that strengthen stomach muscles
    b. Maintaining good posture
    c. Sleeping on your stomach
    d. Stretching the back muscles

24. A syndrome describing a series of characteristic symptoms that occur prior to menstruation in some women is:
    a. Endometriosis
    b. Fibrocystic breast condition
    c. Premenstrual syndrome
    d. Diabetes

25. A common occupational injury associated with video display terminals is:
    a. Carpal tunnel syndrome
    b. Chronic Fatigue Syndrome
    c. Chronic Epstein-Barr disease
    d. Seasonal affective disorder

26. Chemical substances that dilate blood vessels, increase mucous secretions, cause tissues to swell, and produce other allergy-like symptoms are called:
    a. Allergens
    b. Antibodies
    c. Histamines
    d. Antigens

27. A major cause(s) of exercise-induced asthma is(are):
    a. Cold, dry air
    b. Ragweed and flower blooms
    c. Animal dander
    d. Mold

28. A seizure disorder that is characterized by no convulsions, minor loss of consciousness that may go unnoticed, and a minor twitching of muscles is called:
    a. Jacksonian seizure
    b. Grand mal seizure
    c. Petit mal seizure
    d. Psychomotor seizure

29. Diverticulosis occurs when:
    a. The intestinal walls become inflamed
    b. The intestinal walls become weakened for undetermined reasons and small pea-shaped bulges develop
    c. The pancreas fails to produce enough insulin
    d. Endometrial tissue develops abnormally outside the uterus

30. All of the following are common treatments for PMS, except:
    a. Aspirin
    b. Stress relaxation techniques
    c. Exercise
    d. Decreased intake of complex carbohydrates

Language Enrichment Glossary

In addition to the words in the Key Terms list at the end of the chapter, students listed the following words as difficult to understand. Use the chapter Key Terms list, this list, your dictionary, and teachers and friends to learn the meaning of words you do not understand.

abstinence:	avoidance
acute:	intense
afflicted:	infected
allergen:	substance that causes an allergic reaction
antibodies:	body substance which protects against infections or allergens
antigen:	substance that causes production of antibodies
apparent:	obvious
autoinoculate:	infect yourself
average:	normal, ordinary
bloated:	swollen
bone fusion:	join bones
breach:	cross
celibacy:	no sexual relations
cesarean delivery:	surgical delivery
characterized by:	shown by
clamped:	fastened
confidential:	name kept secret
congenital:	inherited
conquered:	defeated
convened:	gathered
correlate:	associate
cramps:	painful muscle contractions
criteria:	measurements
debilitating:	weakening
definitive:	definite, absolute
despite:	in spite of
dilated:	expanded
dirty blow:	unfair behaviour
discriminate:	negative behaviour towards people because they belong to a particular group
disoriented:	confused, lost
dissuade:	persuade not to do something
ducts:	tubes
empowering:	giving a sense of worth
eradicated:	eliminated
erosive:	erodes, deteriorates
etiology:	origin, cause
exacerbate:	make worse
excision:	cut out
excruciatingly:	agonizingly, intensely

extensive:	broad, thorough
fossil evidence:	proof found in old rocks
functional mobility:	ability to move
geared towards:	directed to, focussed on
generated:	created
grave:	serious
hypersensitivity:	overreaction
incidence:	frequency
inflamed:	irritated, red, swollen
inflammation:	swelling, infection
inhalers:	medical breath sprays to improve breathing
inherent:	inherited, built in
inheritance:	inherited from ancestors
inhospitable:	not welcoming
insidious:	not obvious
intractable:	stubborn
irrespective:	regardless
itchy:	skin irritation, needs scratching
jaundice:	liver disease
judicious:	careful
lactose intolerance:	unable to digest milk products
lanky:	tall, thin
lodging:	sticking, attaching
longevity:	number of years to live
maladies:	illnesses
menstruating:	monthly bleeding cycles
midline:	middle of the body
monogamous:	sexual relations with only one partner
nauseated:	sick to the stomach
noninvasive:	not damaging
old standby:	traditional, reliable
onset:	beginning
overt:	obvious, easy to see
overtaxed:	overburdened
overzealous:	trying too hard
particulate matter:	tiny airborne particles
plagued:	bothered by
plateaued:	leveled off
plausible:	believable
precipitating event:	cause
precursor:	beginning
prevalent:	common
probability:	likelihood
prognosis:	expectation of recovery
progressive damage:	worsening, spreading

prompting:	causing
pulsating:	pounding, throbbing
pus:	fluid from infection
radiating:	spreading
rationale:	reason
relapse:	occur again
remission:	disappearance
retraction:	pull back
risk factor:	associated danger, cause
secretion:	discharge, leak
seizure:	convulsion
shafts:	long part
spitting up:	coughing up blood
sporadic:	irregular, periodic
static positions:	held in one place without moving
stunning:	surprising, amazing
subjective:	opinion of the individual
substantiated by:	supported by
surpassed:	opinion of the individual
synthetic:	artificial substance
take hold:	become established
teeming:	covered by
the like:	similar things
theorize:	propose
throw caution to the winds:	behave carelessly
trivialized:	treated as unimportant
trunk:	torso, upper body
turf wars:	disagreements over responsibilities
undue:	excessive
upbringing:	how we were raised
validated:	confirmed, proved
vector:	insects or animals carrying diseases
verifies:	proves
warming up:	stretching muscles before exercise
wheezing:	breathing difficulty
would-be:	attempted

CHAPTER 14
Life's Transitions: The Aging Process

Chapter Overview

Aging is defined as the patterns of life changes that occur in members of all species as they grow older. Discrimination against people based on age is known as ageism. When directed against the elderly, this type of discrimination means social ostracism and negative portrayals for older people. A developmental task approach to life-span changes tends to reduce the potential for ageism. The study of gerontology explores the reasons for aging and the ways in which people cope with and adapt to this process. Gerontologists have identified several types of age-related characteristics to determine a person's life-stage development. Biological age refers to the relative age or condition of the person's organs and body systems. Psychological age is a person's adaptive capacities, such as coping abilities and intelligence. Social age refers to a person's habits and roles relative to society's expectations. Legal age is based on chronological years and is used to determine such things as voting rights and eligibility for Social Security. Functional age is used to compare to others of a similar age. People aged 65 to 74 are classified as young-old; those aged 75 to 84 are the middle-old group; and those 85 and over are classified as the old-old.

People age 65 and older made up 12 percent of Canada's population in 1991; by 2036 they are projected to make up 23 percent of the population. The swelling numbers of elderly will have a growing impact on our society in terms of economy, health care, housing, and ethical considerations.

Two broad groups of theories, biological and psychosocial, explain aging. Biological theories include the wear-and-tear theory, the cellular theory, the autoimmune theory, and the genetic mutation theory. The psychosocial theories of Erikson and Peck both stress the incorporation of age-related factors into lifelong behaviour patterns. Both models stress that successful aging involves maintaining emotional as well as physical well-being.

As we grow older, physical changes occur in the skin, bones and joints, head features, the urinary tract, the heart and lungs, the senses, sexual function, and regulation of body temperature. Stereotypes exist about the decline of cognitive aspects of aging. In reality, intelligence does not decline with age, although the elderly may have some problems with short-term memory. Those who have developed self-confidence, self-reliance, healthy attitudes, and effective coping mechanisms typically lead active lives in their old age. But for those who do experience mental and emotional problems, the most common are depression, senility, and Alzheimer's disease.

Health challenges of the elderly include alcohol abuse, prescription drug use and over-the-counter drug interactions, concern about vitamins and mineral supplements, and caregiving issues.

Dying is the process of decline in body functions resulting in the death of an organism. Death can be defined as the "final cessation of the vital functions" and also refers to a state in which these functions are "incapable of being restored." Various phases of biological death include cell death, local death, somatic death, apparent death, functional death, and brain death. We can look at our attitudes toward death on a continuum. At one end, death is viewed as the mortal enemy of humankind. At the other end of the continuum death is accepted and even welcomed. Most of us perceive ourselves to be in the middle of this continuum. Pervasive death denial has characterized our society's response to death, however, it appears that this attitude is changing.

Thanatology is the study of death and dying. Kubler-Ross identified five psychological stages that terminally ill patients often experience: denial, anger, bargaining, depression, and acceptance. However, subsequent research has shown that the experiences of persons who are dying are not that specific and vary from person to person. Social death is an irreversible situation in which a person is not treated like an active member of society. The need for social support does not diminish in the face of death, and may, in fact, increase. Thousands of reports have been given by people who almost died or were actually pronounced dead but subsequently recovered. The descriptions associated with being near death have many common elements, including the phases of resistance, life review, and transcendence. Bereavement is defined as the loss or deprivation experienced by a survivor when a loved one dies. Because relationships vary in type and intensity, reactions to losses also vary. When a person experiences a loss that cannot be openly acknowledged, publicly mourned, or socially supported, coping may be much more difficult. Grief work is the process of integrating the reality of the loss with everyday life and learning to feel better. Social and emotional support for the bereaved in the aftermath of death is supported by many cultures. Typically, however, there is little support for many other significant losses in life. These quasi-death experiences resemble death in that they involve separation, termination, loss, and a change in identity or self-perception. If grief results from these losses, the pattern of the grief response will probably be similar to responses to death.

There are different types of terminal care available today. An increasing number of people are considering the hospice philosophy as an acceptable alternative to modern "high-tech" death. The primary goals of the hospice program are to relieve the dying person's pain, to offer emotional support to the dying person and loved ones, and to restore a sense of control to the dying person, the family, and friends. Many people prefer to go to a hospital to die. Others choose to die at home, without the intervention of medical staff or life-prolonging equipment. Each dying person and his or her family should decide as early as possible what type of terminal care is most desirable and feasible. Funerals assist survivors of the deceased in coping with their loss. Preplanning of funerary details reduces the stress on survivors and is becoming more acceptable in our culture. Decisions should be made in advance about the issue of wills and organ donation.

The right to die, rational suicide, and euthanasia are all controversial concepts in the study of death and dying. Many people today believe that they have the right to die if they have a terminal condition and their existence is dependent on mechanical life support devices or artificial feeding or hydration systems. As long as a person is conscious and competent, he or she has the legal right to refuse treatment, even if this decision will hasten death. However, when a person is in a coma or is otherwise incapable of speaking on his or her behalf, medical personnel and administrative policy will dictate treatment. The living will was developed to assist in solving conflicts among these people and agencies. Thousands of terminally ill people decide to kill themselves rather than endure constant pain and slow decay. The issue of rational suicide involves ethical, moral, and legal issues. Dyathanasia involves someone playing a passive role in the death of a terminally ill person. Euthanasia involves a person or organization taking an active role to hasten the death of a terminally ill person.

Learning Objectives

1. Review the definition of aging, and explain the related concepts of biological age, psychological age, social age, legal age, and functional age.
2. Explain the impact on society of the growing population of the elderly, including considerations of economics, health care, housing and living arrangements, and ethical and moral issues.

3. Discuss the biological and psychosocial theories of aging and examine how knowledge of these theories may have an impact on your own aging process.

4. Identify the major physiological changes that occur as a result of the aging process.

5. Discuss the unique health challenges faced by the elderly.

6. Describe death using different criteria and evaluate why people deny death.

7. Discuss the stages of the grieving process and describe several strategies for coping more effectively with death.

8. Review the decisions that are necessary when someone is dying or has died, including hospice care, funeral arrangements, wills, and organ donation.

9. Describe the ethical concerns that arise from the concepts of the right to die and rational suicide.

Key Terms

Fill in a brief definition to help you remember these terms.

aging _____

ageism _____

gerontology _____

young-old _____

middle-old _____

old-old _____

osteoporosis_____

urinary incontinence _____

cataracts_____

glaucoma_____

senility_____

Alzheimer's disease_____

comorbidity_____

respite care _____

dying _____

death _____

electroencephalogram (EEG) _____

thanatology _____

social death _____

bereavement _____

disenfranchised grief_____

grief_____

mourning_____

grief work _____

quasi-death experiences _____

hospice _____

intestate _____

holographic will _____

testator_____

self-deliverance _____

dyathanasia _____

euthanasia _____

Critical Thinking Exercises

1. Pam wonders about her grandmother's inability to remember where she went shopping yesterday, while she can clearly recall the details of when she came to Brandon as a child 75 years ago. Explain this phenomenon among the elderly.

2. Among the changes associated with the aging process discussed in the text, which give you the most concern? Why?

3. You are a reporter assigned to cover a situation where a jet lost all power and fell over 10,000 feet before one engine regained power, allowing the jet to land safely. What do you expect the passengers will describe as they recount their near-death experiences?

4. Ellen is concerned about her husband, whose father just died, and with whom he was very close. What common grief reactions can she expect to observe in her husband?

5. Dominic and Sarah's young children are affected by the death of their grandfather. How should they talk with their children about coping with their bereavement?

6. Felicia's brother is conscious and competent, but he has several vital organs that are about to give out. The doctors plan to put him on artificial life support. Without artificial life support, he cannot survive. Can he legally refuse treatment? Why or why not?

Critical Thinking Activity: A Look at Funeral Homes

Funeral rituals tell a lot about our culture's view of death. Collect and review written information from three funeral homes concerning services offered and costs involved. Then consider the following questions:

1. What do the materials suggest about the importance of a funeral?
2. What role does a funeral serve?
3. How much will a funeral cost?
4. What are the advantages of preplanning a funeral?
5. Does it make you uncomfortable to review this information? Why or why not?

General Review Questions

Short Answer

1. What is the study of gerontology?
2. Distinguish between the young-old, middle-old, and old-old.
3. Identify risk factors for developing osteoporosis.
4. What are the three stages of Alzheimer's disease?
5. What is "social death"?
6. Define disenfranchised grief and provide examples of losses that may lead to such grief.
7. What is the objective of hospice programs?
8. What is a living will?

1. The study of the individual and collective aging processes:
    a. Ageology
    b. Gerontology
    c. Genealogy
    d. Archeology

2. A person's habits and roles relative to society's expectations refers to his or her:
    a. Functional age
    b. Psychological age
    c. Legal age
    d. Social age

3. A term used to describe loss of memory and judgment and orientation problems occurring in a small percentage of the elderly is:
    a. Senility
    b. Depression
    c. Psychosis
    d. Schizophrenia

4. One of the most common forms of dementia for the elderly is:
    a. Alzheimer's disease
    b. Incontinence
    c. Depression
    d. Psychosis

5. The "young-old" are people who are:
    a. 55-64 years of age
    b. 65-74 years of age
    c. 75-84 years of age
    d. 85 years or older

6. According to the cellular theory:
    a. Aging is caused by the human body wearing out
    b. Aging is caused by the body's cells having reached the end of their reproductive cycle
    c. Aging is caused by the decline of the body's immunological system
    d. Aging is caused by an increased number of cells exhibiting unusual or different characteristics with increased age

7. As the mind ages:
    a. Short-term memory fluctuates on a daily basis
    b. The ability to remember events from past decades remains unchanged
    c. The elderly are extremely heterogeneous
    d. All of the above

8. To reduce age-related risks, it is important to:
    a. Keep active mentally
    b. Learn to accept help when needed
    c. Have regular medical checkups
    d. All of the above

9. Art is now in his 70s and has noticed that his hearing seems to have changed. What change(s) may have occurred?
    a. His ability to hear high-frequency consonants may have diminished
    b. His ability to distinguish extreme ranges of sound
    c. His ability to distinguish normal conversational tones
    d. Both a and b

10. With age, all of the following occur except:
    a. Earlobes get fatter and grow longer
    b. Overall head circumference increases
    c. Brain size increases
    d. The skull becomes thicker

11. A clouding of the eye lens is called:
    a. Cataracts
    b. Glaucoma
    c. Colorblindness
    d. Astigmatism

12. During menopause, women may experience:
    a. Hot flashes
    b. Weight gain
    c. The development of facial hair
    d. All of the above

13. Your grandmother has suddenly been acting strange. She has been disoriented, erratic, and cannot make a cup of coffee. What may be causing her to behave so strangely?
    a. She may be developing an age-related disorder (i.e., dementia)
    b. She may be having an adverse reaction to OTC drugs
    c. She may be having an adverse reaction to a prescription medication
    d. All of the above

14. The inability to control urination is called:
    a. Osteoporosis
    b. Vital capacity
    c. Urinary incontinence
    d. None of the above

15. A chronic condition involving changes in nerve fibers of the brain that results in mental deterioration is called:
    a. Alzheimer's disease
    b. Presenile dementia
    c. Parkinson's disease
    d. Senility

16. Dying is:
    a. The final cessation of the vital functions of the body
    b. An irreversible situation in which a person is laid to rest
    c. The process of decline in body functions resulting in the death of an organism
    d. The cessation of electrical activity in the brain

17. Brain death occurs when:
    a. There is no response even to painful stimuli
    b. There is no movement for a continuous hour after observation by a physician and no breathing after three minutes off a respirator
    c. The pupils are fixed and dilated
    d. All of the above

18. Angela's grandmother is dying but she keeps assuring her sisters that their grandmother will be okay and will be coming home soon. Angela is most likely experiencing:
    a. Grief
    b. Mourning
    c. Death denial
    d. Bereavement

19. The stage of grief that is characterized by the dying person resolving to be a better person in return for an extension of life is called:
    a. Denial
    b. Anger
    c. Bargaining
    d. Depression

20. An irreversible situation in which a person is not treated like an active member of society is called:
    a. Local death
    b. Functional death
    c. Social death
    d. Somatic death

21. Bereavement is:
    a. Mental distress caused by a loss that cannot be openly acknowledged, publicly mourned, or socially supported
    b. Loss or deprivation experienced by a survivor when a loved one dies
    c. A culturally sanctioned display of grief
    d. Mental distress that occurs in reaction to the loss of a loved one

22. Extramarital lovers who find it difficult to mourn the death of their lover because of societal stigmas may experience:
    a. Bereavement
    b. Bereavement displacement
    c. Disenfranchised grief
    d. Denial

23. Saul has experienced many losses in his life, including the loss of his wife, friends, and children. His gloomy outlook and disturbing behavior patterns may be symptomatic of:
    a. An age-associated dementia
    b. Self-pity
    c. Bereavement overload
    d. Depression

24. The death of a child:
    a. Is considered a major tragedy
    b. May cause surviving children to be emotionally abandoned by their parents
    c. May cause surviving children to feel uncomfortable talking about death
    d. All of the above

25. May has not dated anyone for the past year since her fiancée died and has visited his grave every week. Her actions may be described as:
    a. Mourning
    b. Grief
    c. Death affiliation
    d. Death expectations

26. Funerals serve the purpose of:
    a. Maximizing the quality of life of the survivors
    b. Relieving a dying person' pain
    c. Assisting survivors of the deceased in coping with their loss
    d. Keeping the memory of the deceased alive to the family and friends

27. Burial vaults are:
    a. Concrete or metal containers that hold the casket
    b. The actual container for the body or remains
    c. A funeral ritual in which the embalmed body is viewed
    d. Above ground burial sites

28. An abduction or kidnapping, a divorce, a move to a distant place, and the loss of a romance are examples of:
    a. Quasi-death experiences
    b. Grief
    c. Disenfranchised grief
    d. Mourning

29. The study of death and dying is called:
    a. Thanatology
    b. Gerontology
    c. Kublerology
    d. Social death

30. The form of "mercy killing" in which life-prolonging treatments or interventions are not offered or withheld, thereby allowing a terminally ill person to die naturally is called:
    a. Self-deliverance
    b. Euthanasia
    c. Dyathanasia
    d. Suicide

Language Enrichment Glossary

In addition to the words in the Key Terms list at the end of the chapter, students listed the following words as difficult to understand. Use the chapter Key Terms list, this list, your dictionary, and teachers and friends to learn the meaning of words you do not understand.

ageist:	prejudice, based on age
agonizing:	painful, difficult
ailment:	disease
alienation:	isolation

alleviation:	reduced, soothed
anticipate:	predict ahead of time
apathy:	indifferent, lack of interest
apprehension:	anxiety, worry
arduous:	hard, difficult
argumenting:	increasing, adding to
autoimmune:	immune system attacking itself
bedridden:	confined to bed
beset:	bothered by
bizarre:	extremely unusual
burden:	responsibility
cessation:	ending
chronological:	number of years
coexist:	live together
cognitive ability:	thinking ability
compensating:	making up for
comprehensive:	thorough, inclusive
contemporaries:	colleagues
contend:	deal with
contestable:	opposed, debated
controversy:	disagreement
curtailed:	decreased or ended
designated:	specified, chosen
deteriorate:	break down
differentiated:	separated
dignified:	honourable, respectful
diminishing:	decreasing
disenfranchised:	to take away a right or privilege
disproportionately:	more than expected
dissident:	someone who disagrees with the majority
dose:	prescribed amount
dowager's hump:	large bump at top of back
dysfunction:	unhealthy relationships
earlobes:	bottom part of the ear
ecstasy:	great joy
embalmed:	treated with chemicals to preserve, slow decay
embraced:	enthusiastic agreement
endocrinologist:	one who studies glands
estrogen:	a female hormone
ethical dilemmas:	moral puzzles, difficulties
euphemism:	gentler word for offensive word
euthanasia:	helping one who wants to die
evolved:	developed, resulted
exile:	to be sent away from
extension:	lengthening

facilitate:	make easier
false reassurance:	untrue encouragement
farsightedness:	inability to see close objects clearly
fixed and dilated:	staring and expanded
fortified:	strengthened
futile:	hopeless, useless
gerontologist:	one who studies aging
humane:	kind, merciful
imminent:	approaching
immobilized:	unable to move
immune system:	body's protection system
impending:	upcoming
impersonal:	detached impartial
in accordance with:	agrees with
inconceivable:	unimaginable
indicator:	evidence, a sign
individually characteristic:	associated with one individual
inevitable:	unavoidable
infinity:	endless, limitless future
inflammatory:	causing swelling and irritation
insomnia:	inability to sleep
integrate:	combine, unite
interdisciplinary:	from several different specialties
intrinsic:	natural, inborn
kept under wraps:	hidden
laxative:	something to cause bowel movements
malfunction:	incorrect functioning
mediated:	outsider helps to solve a problem
medical ethicists:	specialists who decide medical moral problems
megadose:	very large amounts
nonconformists:	people who don't follow common behaviour
obituary:	public death notice
ostracism:	isolation
overburdened:	too much responsibility
paradoxical:	contradictory
pathological:	seen as illness
pegged:	attached
perennial:	constant
pervasive:	widespread
portrayals:	pictures, ideas
postmortem:	after death
predispose:	create a tendency toward
predominant:	significant, primary
prescribed:	assigned, established
privileges:	rights

rational:	logical, thought out
rattle on:	talk endlessly
regimen:	diet or therapy system
remains problematic:	still a problem
reprieve:	delay
resolution:	conclusion
respiratory:	breathing
resuscitative:	trying to revive someone
sag:	droop, hang down
sanctity:	sacredness
scrupulous:	careful, painstaking, precise
self-reliance:	depending on yourself
sensationalized:	used to stimulate strong public curiosity
sensory input:	information perceived through the senses
shunted aside:	pushed away
stunned:	shocked
sullen:	gloomy, sulky
sustained:	experienced, been the receive of
symbolic claims:	unreal demands
terminal:	ending, final
undue:	unnecessary, unreasonable
urinate:	to pass urine
validate:	confirm
vigorous:	energetic

CHAPTER 15
Environmental Health: Thinking Globally, Acting Locally

Chapter Overview

Environmental awareness has grown tremendously since the first Earth Day in April 1970. The most challenging environmental problem is population growth. World population is increasing at unprecedented rates. World population in 1995 was 5.7 billion and this is expected to grow by 90 million people a year for the next 20 years, dropping to about 50 million a year by 2050.

Reducing air pollution is another environmental challenge. Concern about air quality lead Parliament to pass the Clean Air Act in 1970 which was consolidated into the Canadian Environmental Protection Act in 1985. This allowed for the development of standards for six of the most widespread air pollutants sulphur dioxide, particulates, carbon monoxide, nitrogen dioxide, ozone, and lead. Photochemical smog is a brown, hazy mix of particulates and gases that forms when oxygen-containing compounds of nitrogen and hydrocarbons react in the presence of sunlight. Long-term exposure to smog produces serious health risks, particularly for children, the elderly, pregnant women, and people with chronic respiratory disorders. Acid rain is precipitation that has fallen through acidic air pollutants, particularly those containing sulphur dioxides and nitrogen dioxides. More than 95 percent of acid rain originates in human actions, primarily the burning of fossil fuels. The effects of acid rain include damage to lake and pond habitats; the destruction of millions of trees in forests in Europe and North America; respiratory problems; possible hazard to a pregnant woman's unborn child; metals leaching out of the soil and lakes and making their way into water or food supplies, causing cancer in humans who consume the water and food; crop damage; and the destruction of public monuments and structures. Indoor air pollution comes primarily from six sources woodstoves, furnaces, asbestos, passive smoke, formaldehyde, and radon. Pollution is depleting the earth's protective ozone layer. Pollution is causing a global warming trend, which adversely affects agriculture and human health. The use of renewable resources, such as solar, wind, and water power as the providers of most of the world's energy as well as shifting away from automobile as the primary source of transportation will reduce air pollution significantly.

There are two general types of water pollution — point source and nonpoint source. Major categories of point source pollutants are sewage treatment plants and industrial facilities. Nonpoint pollutants result from a variety of human land use practices, such as soil erosion and sedimentation, construction wastes, and sewage sludge. Most chemicals designed to dissolve grease and oil are called organic solvents. Organic solvents work their way into the water supply in different ways. After a while, the chemicals leach into the groundwater system. A related group of toxic substances contains chlorinated hydrocarbons, such as the polychlorinated biphenyls and the dioxins.

Noise pollution affects our hearing. Symptoms of noise-related distress include disturbed sleep patterns, headaches, and tension. Short-term exposure reduces productivity, concentration levels, and attention spans, and may affect mental and emotional health. Prolonged exposure to some noises results in hearing loss.

By 1993, 91 percent of the population had access to recycling programs, and 45 percent had hazardous waste programs. Experts believe that as much as 90 percent of our trash is ultimately recyclable.

Ionizing radiation is produced by photons having high enough energy to ionize atoms. Nonionizing radiation is produced by photons associated with lower-energy portions of the electromagnetic spectrum. The disposal and storage of radioactive wastes created by nuclear power plants and the possibility of reactor core meltdown pose serious threats to the environment.

Learning Objectives

1. Identify the problems associated with current levels of global population growth.
2. Discuss the major causes of air pollution, including photochemical smog and acid rain, and the global consequences of the accumulation of greenhouse gases and of ozone depletion.
3. Identify sources of water pollution and the specific chemical contaminants often found in water.
4. Describe the physiological consequences of noise pollution.
5. Distinguish between municipal solid waste and hazardous waste.
6. Discuss the health concerns associated with ionizing and nonionizing radiation.

Key Terms

Fill in a brief definition to help you remember these terms.

sulphur dioxide _____

particulates _____

carbon monoxide_____

nitrogen dioxide_____

ozone _____

lead _____

hydrocarbons_____

photochemical smog _____

temperature inversion _____

acid rain_____

leach _____

asbestos _____

formaldehyde_____

radon _____

chlorofluorocarbons (CFCs). greenhouse gases _____

point source pollutants _____

nonpoint source pollutants _____

leachate _____

polychlorinated biphenyls (PCBs) _____

dioxins_____

pesticides_____

municipal solid waste _____

hazardous waste _____

ionizing radiation _____

radiation absorbed doses (rads)_____

nonionizing radiation _____

meltdown_____

Critical Thinking Exercises

1. How can you reduce the possibility of ingesting lead if it does exist in your home's water system?
2. Michael and Ellen live near a subway. What symptoms of noise-related distress might they experience?
3. Suppose you are debating on the safety of nuclear power plants. Present an argument on how nuclear power plants are a threat to the environment.
4. Suppose that you are on a committee sponsoring Earth Day. What ways would you try to raise public awareness about the environment and how do you propose to try to carry this attitude over into their personal lives?

Critical Thinking Activity: Bringing Environmental Hazards Home

There are certain global environmental problems, and other environmental problems which are more local in nature.

Working through federal, provincial and especially local officials, determine the greatest single environmental hazard in your own community?

Then answer the following questions:

1. What is the greatest single environmental hazard in your community? Is this hazard known in the community? If not, why not?
2. What community efforts are already underway to combat this hazard?
3. What governmental efforts are already underway to combat this hazard?
4. What would be the costs and benefits if this environmental hazard was eliminated?

General Review Questions

Short Answer

1. What is the concept of zero population growth?
2. Identify sources of air pollution.
3. What are sources of acid rain? What are its consequences?
4. Identify six sources of indoor air pollution.
5. What are the consequences of global warming?
6. Identify and define two general sources of water pollution.
7. Distinguish between municipal solid waste and hazardous waste.

Multiple Choice

1 . The world population is expected to grow by approx.____ million people a year for the next 30 years.
    a. 90
    b. 20
    c. 100
    d. 40

2. What course(s) of action for controlling population growth are advocated by proponents?
    a. Zero population growth
    b. Limit family size to only one offspring per couple
    c. Limit family size to only two offspring per couple
    d. Both a and c

3. Sulfur dioxide, a yellowish-brown gas, can:
    a. Aggravate heart and lung disease
    b. Corrode metals
    c. Impair visibility
    d. All of the above

4. The principle source of hydrocarbons is(are):
    a. Automobile engines
    b. Industrial paints
    c. Coal-burning plants
    d. All of the above

5. A weather condition occurring when a layer of cool air is trapped under a layer of warmer air and prevents the air from circulating, is called:
    a. Greenhouse effect
    b. Ozone
    c. Temperature inversion
    d. Photochemical smog

6. Precipitation that has fallen through acidic air pollutants, particularly those containing sulfur dioxides and nitrogen dioxides is known as:
    a. Ozone
    b. Acid rain
    c. Photochemical smog
    d. Temperature inversion

7. A substance that separates into stringy fibers, lodges in lungs and can cause lung cancer is:
   a. Asbestos
   b. Particulate matter
   c. Radon
   d. Formaldehyde

8. Chlorofluorocarbons, chemicals that contribute to the depletion of the ozone layer, are found in:
   a. Refrigerators
   b. Air conditioners
   c. Various foam products
   d. All of the above

9. How much of the earth is covered with water?
   a. 15%
   b. 45%
   c. 60%
   d. 75%

10. Industrial chemicals that can cause cancer and are used in high voltage electrical equipment, such as transformers, are known as:
    a. Dioxins
    b. Polychlorinated biphenyls (PCB's)
    c. Pesticides
    d. Trichlorethylene (TCE)

11. Municipal solid waste contains:
    a. Containers and packaging
    b. Durable goods
    c. Industrial wastes
    d. All of the above

12. The only way to reduce air pollution significantly is:
    a. Increase reliance on alternative energy sources such as windmills
    b. To ban the use of chlorofluorocarbons
    c. To require that all automobiles be converted to electricity
    d. Shift away from automobiles as the primary source of transportation

13. The recommended maximum "safe" dosage of radiation is:
    a. 0.5 rads to 5 rads per year
    b. 2.5 rads to 35 rads per year
    c. 50 rads to 60 rads per year
    d. 100 rads to 2OO rads per year

14. Radiation produced by photons having energy high enough to ionize atoms is called:
    a. Radioactive emissions
    b. Nuclear energy
    c. Fission
    d. Ionizing radiation

15. The most predominant greenhouse gas is:
    a. Lead
    b. Formaldehyde
    c. Carbon dioxide
    d. Chlorofluorocarbons

16. The bulk of the population growth is in:
    a. Eastern Europe
    b. Developing countries in urban areas
    c. The South American rain forests
    d. The United States

17. The reason large families are desired in many developing countries is:
    a. High infant mortality rates
    b. Children are viewed as " social security"
    c. The low economic status of women
    d. All of the above

18. The single biggest contributor towards zero population growth is:
    a. Institutionalized birth control with methods such as Depo-provera and Norplant
    b. Mass sterilization
    c. Education
    d. Abortion

19. The single greatest source of acid rain is:
    a. Burning of fossil fuels
    b. Grazing animal flatulence
    c. Chemical pollutants
    d. Wood stove smoke

20. Exposure to formaldehyde can cause which of the following health problems?
    a. Respiratory problems
    b. Fatigue
    c. Cancer
    d. All of the above

21. The most noticeable adverse effect(s) of exposure to smog is(are):
    a. Difficulty breathing
    b. Burning eyes
    c. Nausea
    d. All of the above

22. Chemicals that are designed to kill insects, rodents, plants, and fungi are called:
    a. Pesticides
    b. Polychlorinated biphenyls
    c. Dioxins
    d. Benzene

23. Chemicals that contribute to the depletion of the ozone layer are called:
    a. Ozone
    b. Chlorofluorocarbons
    c. Hydrocarbons
    d. Carbon monoxide

24. Which of the following is not a greenhouse gas?
    a. Carbon dioxide
    b. Radon
    c. Ground level ozone
    d. Methane

25. The two major categories of point source pollutants are:
    a. Sewage treatment plants and landfills
    b. Sewage treatment plants and industrial facilities
    c. Acid mine leakage and landfills
    d. Industrial facilities and landfills

26. The most common way to detect the presence of petroleum products in the water supply is:
    a. To test for benzene
    b. To test for leaching in groundwater
    c. To calculate the number of miscarriages and cancer cases in the community
    d. To test for carbon monoxide

27. Long-term exposure to pesticides has been linked to:
    a. Birth defects
    b. Liver and kidney damage
    c. Nervous system disorders
    d. All of the above

28. A symptom of noise-related distress is:
    a. Decreased blood pressure
    b. Increased productivity
    c. Decreased cholesterol levels
    d. Increased secretion of adrenaline

29. Solid waste that, due to its toxic properties, poses a health hazard to humans or to the environment is called:
    a. Municipal waste
    b. Environmental waste
    c. Hazardous waste
    d. Toxic waste

30. The most dangerous type of radiation is:
    a. Alpha particles
    b. Beta particles
    c. Gamma rays
    d. All of the above are equally dangerous

Language Enrichment Glossary

In addition to the words in the Key Terms list at the end of the chapter, students listed the following words as difficult to understand. Use the chapter Key Terms list, this list, your dictionary, and teachers and friends to learn the meaning of words you do not understand.

aggravates:	makes worse
beget:	conceive
cling:	stick to
coincide:	happen at the same time
complacency:	contentment
degradation:	deterioration
depleting:	using up
diagnostic:	used to diagnose health problems
dire:	serious
discrete:	specific, separate
dissipate:	scatter, get rid of
emissions:	something sent out of
emit:	send out
hinders:	slows or stops
inequitable:	unfair
leach:	soak
mutation:	change from normal
obscure:	hide, limit
precursor:	occurs before
predominant:	most frequent
probe:	investigation
proponents:	supporters
rely:	depend on
rooted:	based
seep:	leak
shifting:	moving
smelters:	metal refineries
susceptibility:	tendency toward

CHAPTER 16
Consumerism: Selecting Health-Care Products and Services

Chapter Overview

Being an informed consumer will help you obtain optimal health care in a cost effective manner. Perhaps the single greatest difficulty that we face as health consumers is the sheer magnitude of choices available to us. Wise consumers use every means available to them to ensure that they are acting responsibly in their own health choices.

A recent concept in health consumerism is that the patient is the primary health care provider, which means knowing your own body and its signals, and taking action to stop the progression of illness or injury or to improve your overall health. Effective self-care also means knowing when you should need professional medical attention. If you need medical help, you must then identify what type you need and where to obtain it. Knowledge of both allopathic medical specialties and alternative medicine and an awareness of your own criteria for evaluating a health care professional are necessary to make an informed decision. In considering prospective health care providers, you need to take into account the professional educational training they have had.

Allopathic medicine is traditional, Western medical practice; in theory, it is based on scientifically validated methods and procedures. Medical alternatives to traditional medicine are called nonallopathic medicine. Examples of nonallopathic medicine include chiropractic treatment, acupuncture, herbalists and homeopathy, and naturopathy.

There are different types of medical practices available. Physicians in group practice share the same offices, equipment, utility bills, staff costs, and profits. Solo practitioners are doctors who practice independently of other practitioners. Both hospitals and clinics provide a spectrum of health care, including emergency treatment, diagnostic tests and inpatient and outpatient care. Selection of a hospital or clinic will depend on your particular needs, income, insurance coverage, and the availability of services in your community.

Problems of the health care system include cost, access, quality of care, malpractice, fraud and abuse. Factors that contribute to rising health-care costs include excessive administrative costs, duplication of services, half-way technologies, an aging population, the technological imperative, an emphasis on crisis-oriented care, inappropriate utilization of services by consumers, and inflationary reimbursement systems. Your access to health care depends on availability of providers and facilities plus your health status. The Canadian health-care system employs several mechanisms for assuring quality services overall education, licensure, certification/registration, accreditation, peer review, and the legal system of malpractice litigation. Infant mortality rates and life expectancy rates are two commonly used measures of the quality of medical care.

Health care is funded via a single payer system, the federal and provincial governments (Medicare). Health Service Organizations are being explored as a new model of health care.

Learning Objectives

1. Explain when self-diagnosis and self-care are appropriate, when you should seek medical care, and how to assess health professionals.

2. Compare and contrast allopathic and nonallopathic medicine, including the types of treatment that fall into each category.

3. Discuss the types of health care available, including types of medical practices, hospitals, and clinics.

4. Examine the current problems associated with our health-care system, including cost, access, and quality.

5. Describe the objectives of Health Service Organizations.

Key Terms

Fill in a brief definition to help you remember these terms.

spontaneous remission _____

placebo effect _____

allopathic medicine _____

primary care practitioner _____

nurse _____

nonallopathic medicine _____

chiropractic medicine _____

group practice _____

solo practitioner _____

nonprofit (voluntary) hospitals _____

for-profit (proprietary) hospitals _____

outpatient (ambulatory) care _____

Medicare _____

specialty hospitals _____

Critical Thinking Exercises

1. Suppose you have just moved to a new city and need to find a physician. What factors should you consider about a prospective health care provider?

2. Karen has just finished her residency in internal medicine and is deciding whether to join a group practice or to go solo. What should Karen consider in her decision?

3. Suppose you are a hospital administrator and have just been transferred to another hospital. What are your central issues of concern for health care?

Critical Thinking Activity: Selecting A Primary Care Practitioner

There are many criteria for selecting a primary care practitioner. When it comes to those criteria, all doctors are not created equal. Choose three primary care practitioners at random out of the yellow pages. Call their offices and ask for the following information:

a. professional educational training

b. licenses or board certifications held

c. affiliations with medical facilities

d. years of experience

e. weekend and evening office hours

Questions for the Critical Thinker

After compiling this information, reflect on the following questions. Your thoughtful responses will help you in the understanding of consumerism.

1. Have you ever asked these sort of questions before? If not, why not?

2. Was it difficult to ask these questions? Why or why not?

3. How eager were the offices to answer your questions? Do you think that other consumers ask such questions in their search for a primary care practitioner?

4. What conclusions would you make about choice of a primary care practitioner based on the information you received?

5. What other questions or concerns do you have about a primary care practitioner?

General Review Questions

Short Answer

1. People often fall victim to false health claims because they mistakenly believe that a product or provider has helped them. This belief often arises from what two conditions?

2. Identify three examples of nonallopathic alternatives.

3. What problem does Canada have concerning access to health care?

4. What are the underlying principles of Medicare?

Multiple Choice

1. What is the single greatest difficulty that we face as health care consumers?
   a. The limited number of physicians who will accept new patients
   b. Being reimbursed by insurance companies and limited coverage
   c. The sheer magnitude of choices available to consumers
   d. Not knowing the adverse and often unforeseeable effects of medical treatments

2. It is important to seek medical care if experiencing:
   a. Any serious accident or injury
   b. Tingling sensation in the arm accompanied by slurring speech or impaired thought processes
   c. Unexplained sudden weight loss
   d. All of the above

3. A medical practitioner who treats routine ailments, advises on preventive care, gives general medical advice, and makes appropriate referrals when necessary is called a(n):
   a. General practitioner
   b. Family primary provider
   c. Primary care practitioner
   d. Primary family physician

4. Medical alternatives to traditional medicine are called:
   a. Allopathic medicine
   b. Nonallopathic medicine
   c. Managed medicine
   d. Allied medicine

5. A midlevel practitioner trained to handle most standard cases of care is called a:
   a. Physician's assistant
   b. Nurse practitioner
   c. Licensed Practical nurse
   d. Physician's Assistant

6. Medical alternatives to traditional medicine are known as:
   a. Allopathic medicine
   b. Primary medicine
   c- Nonallopathic medicine
   d. Chiropractic medicine

7. The type of medical practice in which a physician renders care to patients independently of other practitioners is called:
   a. Group practice
   b. Single specialty group practice
   c. Solo practitioner
   d. Both a and b

8. Treatments or services that do not require an overnight stay in a hospital are called:
   a. Ambulatory care
   b. Proprietary services
   c. Outpatient care
   d. Both a and c

165

9. Private (for-profit) hospitals are very rare in Canada but those that do exist usually:
   a. offer the same services as nonprofit hospitals
   b. offer specialized services
   c. get the same tax breaks as nonprofit hospitals
   d. offer superior service to patients

10. Hospitals run by religious or other humanitarian groups that reinvest their earnings in the hospital to improve health care are called:
    a. Health maintenance organizations
    b. Outpatient care centers
    c. For-profit hospitals
    d. Nonprofit hospitals

11. Medicare provides coverage for:
    a. Elderly over 65 years of age
    b. All people total and permanently disabled
    c. All people with end-stage renal failure
    d. All of the above

12. Physicians who treat routine ailments, advises on preventive care, gives general medical advice and makes appropriate referrals is called a:
    a. Tertiary care provider
    b. Primary care provider
    c. Secondary care provider
    d. None of the above

13. George has a suspicious growth on his back that his doctor wants to have biopsied. What type of ambulatory facility will he most likely go to for his biopsy?
    a. An emergency center
    b. A surgicenter
    c. A hospital
    d. A cancer treatment center

14. Health insurance is built on the concept of:
    a. Health care is the right of all people
    b. Spreading the risk among a large, diverse group of people
    c. Reducing the risk of catastrophic illness
    d. Providing quality health care coverage for a reasonable cost

15. A new model of health care, currently in place in Ontario, is designed to contain costs while providing improved services and encouraging prevention and shared responsibility is called:
    a. HMO
    b. MBO
    c. HSO
    d. HSM

16. Amanda is having trouble seeing and needs to have new glasses. She would most likely visit an:
    a. Orthodontist
    b. Optometrist
    c. Ophthalmologist
    d. Orthopedist

17. As a result of an automobile accident, Huang had a broken jaw that will require extensive surgical procedures. He will most likely need to see a(n):
    a. Dentist
    b. Orthodontist
    c. Orthopedic surgeon
    d. Oral surgeon

18. Informed consent is the right to have understandable information about:
    a. Side effects of the medical treatment
    b. Benefits of the medical treatment
    c. Available options to the medical treatment
    d. All of the above

19. A medical practice based on scientifically validated methods and procedures whose objective is to heal by countering the patient's symptoms is considered:
    a. Allopathic medicine
    b. Nonallopathic medicine
    c. Osteopathic medicine
    d. Chiropractic medicine

20. A nonallopathic practice that is based on the medicinal qualities of plants or herbs and is based on the theory that the administration of extremely diluted doses of potent natural agents that produce disease symptoms in healthy persons will cure the disease in the sick is called:
    a. Osteopathic medicine
    b. Homeopathic medicine
    c. Chiropractic medicine
    d. Orthopedic medicine

21. Herbal medicine, massage, megavitamins, and energy healing are all types of:
    a. Allopathic medicine
    b. Placebos
    c. Complimentary medicine
    d. Chiropractic medicine

22. All of the following are true about nonprofit hospitals, except:
    a. They are traditionally run by religious or other humanitarian groups
    b. They routinely transfer indigent or uninsured patients to public hospitals
    c. They generally reinvest their earnings in the hospital for the purpose of improving health care
    d. They have often cared for patients whether or not they could pay

23. Hospitals that provide a return on earnings to the investors who own them are called:
    a. Group practices
    b. Nonprofit hospitals
    c. For-profit hospitals
    d. Ambulatory care centers

24. In recent years, how much of the gross national produce (GNP) has been spent on health care?
    a. 5%
    b. 15%
    c. 9.5%
    d. 35%

25. A Chinese medical treatment that has been shown to improve quality of life and improve or cure certain health conditions is:
    a. Massage
    b. Accupressure
    c. Homeopathy
    d. Herbal medicine

26. This type of hospital is likely to have a helicopter landing pad attached:
    a. A Children's hospital
    b. An ambulatory care centre
    c. A trauma centre
    d. All hospitals have these

27. A type of health insurance that provides a wide range of covered health benefits for a fixed amount prepaid by the employee, employer, or Medicare is called:
    a. A prepaid group practice
    b. A health maintenance organization
    c. A preferred provider organization
    d. A public plan insurance

28. Ophthalmologists specialize in the medical and surgical care of:
    a. The eyes
    b. The heart and blood vessels
    c. The female reproductive system
    d. Cancerous growths and tumors

29. Cost-control procedures used by health insurers to coordinate treatment are called:
    a. Managed care
    b. Deductibles
    c. Copayments
    d. Coinsurance

30. The type of medical practice in which a group of physicians combine resources, sharing offices, equipment, and staff costs is called:
    a. Solo practice
    b. Group practice
    c. Fee-for-service practice
    d. For-profit practice

Language Enrichment Glossary

In addition to the words in the Key Terms list at the end of the chapter, students listed the following words as difficult to understand. Use the chapter Key Terms list, this list, your dictionary, and teachers and friends to learn the meaning of words you do not understand.

access:	admission
adamantly:	in a determined manner
adverse:	negative, harmful
allotted:	assigned, set aside
amend:	alter
arsenal:	storehouse, stockpile
attribute:	characteristic
charlatans:	fakes, imposters
condescending:	done with a superior manner
consensus process:	decision process where all attempt to agree
dilemma:	problem, puzzle
divert:	turn aside
drastic:	extreme
dubious:	doubtful, untrustworthy
efficacious:	useful
evolve:	develop
experiential background:	experience
exploit:	take advantage of
fraud:	deceit, cheating
freestanding:	existing alone
generic names:	general names for a category of things
gimmicks:	tricks
ground swell:	public opinion
hangs tenuously:	connected loosely and about to fall
HSO:	Health Service Organization
humanitarian:	volunteer social assistance
hypothetical:	imaginary
imperative:	essential, necessary
in flux:	changing
incremental:	small step by step
indigent:	poor, without resources
infinite:	endless
intimidated:	scared
mainstreaming:	to not isolate, to include with the majority
mandated:	ordered
markedly:	significantly
maze:	confusing puzzle
means:	methods, resources
multifactorial:	including many reasons
pluralistic:	a combination
primary care physician:	general care doctor
proactive:	initiate activity
prohibited:	prevented
prospective:	expected
sheer magnitude:	large size
streamlining:	simplifying
substantiated:	proved
trendy:	popular, stylish
unscrupulous:	unethical, without morals
utilization review:	review of use of services
viable options:	workable choices
warrant:	require

ANSWERS TO
GENERAL REVIEW QUESTIONS

CHAPTER 1:   PROMOTING HEALTHY BEHAVIOUR CHANGE

Short Answer

1. Physical, Social, Mental, Emotional, Environmental, and Spiritual Health.

2. Prevention is taking positive actions now to avoid even becoming sick; primary, secondary, and tertiary prevention

3. Predisposing, enabling, and reinforcing factors.

4. Belief is appraisal of relationship between some object, action, or idea and some attribute of that object, action or idea. Attitude is a relatively stable set of beliefs, feelings, and behavioural tendencies in relation to something or someone.

5. Perceived seriousness of the health problem; perceived susceptibility to the health problem; cues to action.

6. Frequency, duration, seriousness, basis for problem behaviour, antecedents.

Multiple Choice

1. C	6. A	11. A	16. A	21. C	26. B
2. B	7. C	12. B	17. D	22. D	27. B
3. B	8. A	13. D	18. B	23. D	28. D
4. D	9. D	14. A	19. B	24. A	29. A
5. D	10. C	15. A	20. C	25. D	30. D

CHAPTER 2:   PSYCHOSOCIAL HEALTH

Short Answer

1. Four basic types of emotions: those resulting from harm, loss, or threats - those resulting from benefits - borderline emotions of hope and compassion - complex emotions such as grief, disappointment, bewilderment and curiosity

2. They feel good about themselves, feel comfortable with other people, control tension and anxiety, able to meet the demands of life, curb hate and guilt, maintain a positive outlook, enrich the lives of others, cherish the things that make them smile, value diversity, and appreciate nature.

3. Violence; sexual, physical, or emotional abuse; negative behaviors; distrust; anger; dietary deprivation; drug abuse; parental discord; and, other negative characteristics are present; and love security, and unconditional trust are lacking.

4. Hereditary traits, hormonal functioning, physical health status, physical fitness level, and selected elements of mental and emotional health.

5. Family history of suicide, previous suicide attempts, excessive drug and alcohol use, prolonged depression, financial difficulties, serious illness in contemplator or loved ones.

6. Find a support group, complete required tasks, form realistic expectations, take/make time for self, maintain physical health, examine problems and seek help.

7. Phobias, panic attacks and post-traumatic stress disorder.

Multiple Choice

1. A	6. B	11. D	16. B	21. A	26. D
2. B	7. B	12. D	17. C	22. B	27. C
3. C	8. B	13. A	18. A	23. D	28. A
4. D	9. A	14. B	19. A	24. A	29. D
5. B	10. D	15. D	20. D	25. C	30. C

CHAPTER 3   MANAGING STRESS

Short Answer

1. Alarm, Resistance, and Exhaustion.

2. Eustress is considered positive stressful events in one's life and distress is negative stressfull events. Psychosocial factors such as changes, hassles, pressure, inconsistent goals and objectives, conflict, overload and burnout, environmental stressors (i.e., natural and man-made disasters), and self-imposed stress could be considered to be distress. Getting married, going on your first date, getting your driver's license could all be considered eustress

3. Hard-driving, competitive, anxious, time-driven, extremely impatient, angry, and perfectionistic.

4. Control, commitment, and challenge.

5. Increases the predictability of stressful events, fosters coping skills, generates self-talking, encourages confidence about successful outcomes, builds a commitment to personal action and responsibility for an adaptive course of action.

Multiple Choice

1. D	6. D	11. A	16. A	21. D	26. A
2. C	7. A	12. A	17. C	22. D	27. A
3. C	8. A	13. C	18. A	23. D	28. D
4. D	9. D	14. A	19. B	24. C	29. B
5. B	10. D	15. D	20. B	25. A	30. C

CHAPTER 4	**VIOLENCE AND ABUSE**

Short Answer

1. It explains how women can get caught in a downward spiral of abuse and violence without knowing what is happening to them. The phases are: tension building, acute battering, remorse/ reconciliation.

2. Poverty, unemployment, hopelessness, lack of education, inadequate housing, poor parental role models, cultural beliefs that objectify women and empower men to act as aggressors, lack of social support systems, discrimination, ignorance about people who are different, religious selfrighteousness, breakdowns in the criminal justice system, stress and economic uncertainty.

3. Minimization, trivialization, blaming the victim, and "boys will be boys."

4. Gangs provide a sense of belonging to a "family" and economic security.

5. Ask harasser to stop, document harassment, complain to a superior. (Remember that you have not done anything wrong.)

6. Lack of parenting skills, cultural acceptance of corporal punishment and violence within society, stresses including; unwanted child, unsupported single-parent household, absence of social support, financial pressures, unemployment — substance abuse may be another contributing factor

Multiple Choice

1. D	6. D	11. A	16. B	21. D	26. A
2. D	7. D	12. D	17. B	22. D	27. C
3. D	8. D	13. D	18. D	23. A	28. D
4. D	9. D	14. A	19. D	24. A	29. B
5. C	10. B	15. C	20. A	25. B	30. D

Short Answer

1. Approval and a sense of purpose in life, intimacy, social integration, nurturant; assistance reassurance or affirmation of our own worth.

2. All the characteristics of friendship (enjoyment, acceptance, trust, respect, mutual assistance, confiding, understanding, spontaneity) as well as fascination, exclusivity, sexual desire, giving the utmost, being an advocate.

3 . Intimacy, passion, decision/commitment.

4. Females: breast development, enlargement of external genitalia, growth of pubic hair, deposits of fat on hips and buttocks, and fine-textured skin and body hair. Males: growth of facial and body hair, deepening of voice, broadening of shoulders, and harrowing of hips.

5. Excitement/arousal, plateau, orgasm, and resolution. In males: refractory.

6. Can reduce inhibitions to make sexual behaviours less stressful. As a depressant in quantity it can impair erection ability, arousal, and orgasm.

Multiple Choice

1. D	6. D	11. A	16. A	21. B	26. D
2. A	7. C	12. A	17. B	22. D	27. D
3. C	8. D	13. B	18. B	23. B	28. D
4. B	9. C	14. B	19. D	24. B	29. C
5. B	10. C	15. B	20. B	25. A	30. D

CHAPTER 6   **BIRTH CONTROL, PREGNANCY AND CHILDBIRTH**

Short Answer

1 . A viable egg, a viable sperm, and possible access to the egg by the sperm.

2. Tubal ligation and hysterectomy for the female and vasectomy in the male.

3. Missed period, breast tenderness, extreme fatigue, sleeplessness, emotional upset, nausea, and vomiting.

4. Dilation and effacement, transition, pushing (expulsion stage), birth of the baby and delivery of the placenta.

5. Infection, incomplete abortion, excessive bleeding, and cervical and uterine trauma. Also, in second trimester abortions: increased risk of uterine perforation, bleeding, infection, and incomplete abortion because the uterine wall becomes thinner as the pregnancy progresses.

Matching

1.

1.	D	7.	F
2.	G	8.	L
3.	A	9.	E
4.	H	10.	I
5.	C	11.	J
6.	B	12.	K

2.

1.   B   2.   C   3.   A   4.   D

Multiple Choice

1. B	6. C	11. A	16. B	21. D	26. C
2. D	7. D	12. B	17. C	22. D	27. D
3. D	8. C	13. B	18. C	23. A	28. C
4. A	9. D	14. B	19. A	24. D	29. A
5. B	10. D	15. B	20. B	25. B	30. D

CHAPTER 7   NUTRITION

Short Answer

1. A unit of measure that indicates the amount of energy we obtain from a particular food.

2. The process by which foods are broken down and either absorbed or excreted by the body. In the mouth saliva contains enzymes that begin to chemically break down the food — chewing mechanically breaks it into small pieces. Once swallowed the food enters the stomach and is subjected to further chemical and mechanical action. Next the chyme enters the small intestine and is subjected to further chemical and mechanical action — the nutrients found within the food are then absorbed into the bloodstream or excreted.

3. Simple sugars and complex carbohydrates.

4. Protection against: colon and rectal cancer, breast cancer, constipation, diverticulosis, heart disease, diabetes and obesity.

5. HDL's are compounds that facilitate the transport of .cholesterol in the blood to the lover for metabolism and elimination from the body. LDL's are compounds that facilitate the transport of cholesterol in the blood to the body's cells.

6. Saturated fats are unable to hold any more hydrogen in their chemical structure (mostly from animal sources — solid at room temperature) and unsaturated have room for more hydrogen (mostly from plants — liquid at room temperature)

Multiple Choice

1. A	6. B	11. C	16. C	21. B	26. A
2. C	7. C	12. A	17. D	22. C	27. D
3. A	8. B	13. D	18. A	23. D	28. B
4. C	9. C	14. D	19. C	24. B	29. C
5. D	10. B	15. D	20. B	25. D	30. D

CHAPTER 8   MANAGING YOUR WEIGHT

Short Answer

1. Essential fat is necessary for normal physiological functioning of the body - storage fat makes up the remainder of the fat reserves.

2. Ectomorphic: tall, slender frames, generally experience few difficulties with weight control; Endomorphic: rounded, soft appearance, often with a large abdomen and typically a history of weight problems beginning in childhood;

   Mesomorphic: shorter, more muscular, athletic-looking, tendency to gain weight later in life.

3. Hunger is an inborn physiological response to nutritional needs and appetite is a learned response that is tied to an emotional or psychological craving for food that is often unrelated to nutritional need.

4. Age, gender, lean muscle mass, self-protective mechanisms, and stress all influence basal metabolic rate.

5. Determine what triggers your eating behavior, change your triggers, set realistic goals, seek assistance from reputable sources in selecting a dietary plan that is easy to follow and includes adequate amounts of the basic nutrients.

6. Anorexia is an eating disorder characterized by excessive preoccupation with food, self-starvation, and/or extreme exercising to achieve weight loss. Bulimia is characterized by binge eating followed by inappropriate compensating measures taken to prevent weight gain, e.g., self-induced vomiting or use of laxatives.

Multiple Choice

1.	B	6.	B	11.	C	16.	B	21.		26.	D
2.	B	7.	B	12.	A	17.	C	22.		27.	A
3.	C	8.	B	13.	D	18.	B	23.		28.	B
4.	C	9.	A	14.	B	19.	A	24.		29.	D
5.	B	10.	C	15.	A	20.	B	25.		30.	B

Short Answer

1. Combine regular endurance type exercises with a moderate decrease in food intake.

2. Improved cardiorespiratory endurance, bone mass, weight control, health, life span, and physical fitness.

3. Cardiorespiratory endurance, flexibility, muscular strength and muscular endurance.

4. Frequency, intensity and time duration

5. Tension principle, overload principle and the specificity of training principle.

6. Isometric muscle action — force produced without any resulting muscle movement
   Concentric muscle action — force produced while shortening the muscle
   Eccentric muscle action — force produced while lengthening the muscle

7. Plantar Fasciitis, shin splints, runner's knee

8. RICE: Rest, ice, compression, and elevation

Multiple Choice

1.	C	6.	C	11.	A	16.	D	21.	B	26.	C
2.	C	7.	D	12.	B	17.	B	22.	D	27.	B
3.	B	8.	A	13.	B	18.	D	23.	D	28.	A
4.	D	9.	C	14.	A	19.	C	24.	C	29.	C
5.	D	10.	D	15.	B	20.	A	25.	C	30.	B

Short Answer

1. It must have the potential to produce a positive mood change.

2. Four components are: compulsion/obsession, loss of control, negative consequences, and denial.

3. Examples of recreational drugs include: alcohol, tobacco, coffee, and chocolate.

4. Routes of administration include: ingestion, injection, inhalation, inunction and suppositories.

5. Drug misuse is the use of a drug for a purpose for which it was not intended.
   Drug abuse is the excessive use of a drug.

6. Synergism is the interaction of one or more drugs that produces more profound effects than would be expected if the drugs were taken separately. This is most likely to occur when CNS depressants are combined, e.g., alcohol and tranquilizers.

Multiple Choice

1. A	6. C	11. A	16. A	21. D	26. C
2. B	7. C	12. D	17. D	22. C	27. A
3. A	8. C	13. D	18. B	23. B	28. B
4. C	9. D	14. C	19. A	24. A	29. C
5. B	10. D	15. A	20. B	25. B	30. A

Short Answer

1. The alcohol concentration in the drink, the amount of alcohol consumed, the amount of food in the stomach, drinker's size, sex, body build and rate of metabolism, and the person's mood.

2. Developmental delay, sleeping difficulties, hyperactivity, learning disabilities, dyslexia, congestive heart problems, physical deformities and genetourinary problems.

3. Type 1 avoids novelty and harmful situations and are concerned about the thoughts and feelings of others — they have at least one parent who is/was an alcoholic. Type 2 is found in males only and are biological sons of alcoholic fathers who have a history of both violence and drug use. Behaviours are generally opposite to those of Type 1.

4. Smokeless tobacco impairs sense of smell and taste, leads to dental problems including gum disease and halitosis, and may also interfere with absorption of Vitamins and nutrients.

5.   Health benefits of quitting smoking include: reduced risk of stroke, cancers, lung disease, peripheral artery disease, coronary disease, ulcer and low birth weight babies. Reproductive abilities may also improve.

6.   Some of the biological effects of caffeine include: insomnia, headaches, irritability and nervousness.

Multiple Choice

1. A	6. D	11. A	16. A	21. D	26. B
2. A	7. D	12. B	17. B	22. B	27. D
3. D	8. C	13. D	18. C	23. C	28. D
4. C	9. D	14. D	19. C	24. D	29. A
5. B	10. D	15. C	20. B	25. D	30. D

CHAPTER 12   CARDIOVASCULAR DISEASE AND CANCER

Short Answer

1 .   Common forms of cardiovascular disease include: atherosvlerosis, arteriosclerosis, heart attack, angina pectoris, irregular heartbeat (arrhythmia), congestive heart failure, congenital and rheumatic heart disease, and stroke.

2.   Tachycardia is an abnormally fast heartbeat and bradycardia is an abnormally slow heartbeat.

3.   Three main reasons for neglect of symptoms of heart disease by women: 1) physicians may often be gender-biased 2) physicians tend to view male heart disease as a more severe problem 3) women decline major procedures more often than men do.

4.   Benign tumours are generally harmless and non-cancerous tumours generally composed of ordinary-looking cells enclosed in a fibrous shell or capsule, malignant tumours are generally very harmful and are cancerous in nature not usually being enclosed in a protective capsule and can therefore spread to other tissue (metastasis).

5.   Carcinomas, sarcomas, lymphomas and leukemia.

6.   Warning signals include: persistent breast changes such as a lump, thickening, swelling, dimpling, skin irritation, distortion, retraction or scaliness of the nipple, nipple discharge, pain, or tenderness. The risk factors include: being over age 40, having a primary relative who had breast cancer, never having had children, or never having breast-fed a baby, having your first child after the age of 30, early menarche, late age of menopause, and having higher education and socioeconomic status.

7. Symptoms of prostate cancer include: weak or interrupted urine flow, or difficulty starting or stopping the flow, need to urinate frequently, pain or difficulty in urinating, blood in the urine, pain in the lower back, pelvis, or upper thigh.

8. Most common risk factor for oral cancer is tobacco use.

Multiple Choice

1. C	6. C	11. B	16. B	21. A	26. D
2. D	7. D	12. D	17. A	22. B	27. B
3. C	8. B	13. D	18. C	23. C	28. C
4. D	9. A	14. C	19. A	24. A	29. D
5. A	10. B	15. B	20. B	25. C	30. B

CHAPTER 13 INFECTIOUS AND NONINFECTIOUS CONDITIONS

Short Answer

1 . Direct contact, indirect contact, food-borne infection, animal-borne infection, and water-borne infection.

2. Targeting the bodies own tissues and destroying them — e.g. rheumatoid arthritis, lupus and myasthenia gravis.

3. Natural immunity is that which a mother passes to her fetus via the placenta and acquired immunity is that which is from artificial sources such as vaccines.

4. High rates of STI's occur for many reasons: moral and social stigma keep people from getting treatment, casual attitude about sex, many partners, unprotected sex with strangers, ignorance about the infections and symptoms.

5. High risk behaviours include: exchange of body fluids, receiving a blood transfusion prior to 1986, injecting drugs, and mother to infant transmission.

6. Greatest risk is motor vehicle or other accidents.

7. A common, noncancerous condition in which a woman's breasts contain fibrous or fluid-filled cysts.

8. A disease in which the immune system attacks the body producing antibodies that destroy or injure organs such as the kidneys, brain, and heart

Multiple Choice

1. B	6. A	11. A	16. C	21. C	26. C
2. C	7. D	12. C	17. B	22. C	27. A
3. D	8. A	13. B	18. A	23. C	28. C
4. D	9. B	14. A	19. B	24. C	29. B
5. B	10. D	15. B	20. D	25. A	30. D

CHAPTER 14   LIFE'S TRANSITIONS

Short Answer

1. The study of individual and collective aging processes that explores the reasons for aging and the way in which people adapt to this process.

2. young-old - 65-74   middle-old - 75-84   old-old - 85 and over.

3. Gender, age, low bone mass, early menopause, thin, small-framed body, race, lack of calcium, lack of physical activity, cigarette smoking, alcohol and/or caffeine abuse, and heredity.

4. **Stage 1** includes: forgetfulness, memory loss, impaired judgement, increasing inability to handle routine tasks, disorientation, lack of interest in one's surroundings, and depression.
    Stage 2 sees and acceleration of these symptoms plus agitation and restlessness, loss of sensory perception, muscle twitching, and repetitive actions
    Stage 3 is characterized by complete disorientation — becomes completely dependent upon others - identity loss, speech problems — loss of bodily functions

5. Social death is an irreversible situation in which a person is not treated like an active member of society.

6. Disenfranchised grief occurs when a person experiences a loss that cannot be openly acknowledged, publicly mourned, or socially supported, e.g., death of a divorced spouse, death of a secret lover, death of a gay lover.

7. Hospice programs are developed to provide maximum quality to the remaining life for a terminal patient.

8. A living will is a written document in which you can set out your wishes for health care in the event that some time in the future you are unable to consent to treatment.

Multiple Choice

1. B	6. B	11. A	16. C	21. B	26. C
2. D	7. D	12. D	17. D	22. C	27. A
3. A	8. D	13. D	18. C	23. C	28. D
4. A	9. D	14. C	19. C	24. D	29. B
5. B	10. C	15. A	20. C	25. A	30. A

CHAPTER 15	ENVIRONMENTAL HEALTH

Short Answer

1. Only two offspring per couple to stabilize the population.

2. Sulphur dioxide, particulates, carbon monoxide, nitrogen dioxide, ozone, lead and hydrocarbons.

3. Rain, snow, fog — burning of fossil fuels damage lakes, ponds, streams, destruction of trees/forests, aggravates asthma, bronchitis and other respiratory problems, leaching of metals, crop damage (contributes to world hunger), destruction of public buildings and monuments.

4. Woodstoves, furnaces, asbestos, passive smoke, formaldehyde, household chemicals and radon.

5. Increased production of greenhouse gases — ozone causes damage to crops and trees causes much forest decline.

6. Point source pollution is that which arises from a specific location or point, e.g., chemical factory. Non-point source pollution is that which arises from a broad base rather than a specific point, e.g., pesticide runoff from numerous fields into the water table.

7. Municipal solid waste is garbage produced by residential, commercial, institutional and industrial sources that ends up in municipal landfill sites. Hazardous waste is toxic in nature and poses a hazard to humans or the environment.

Multiple Choice

1. B	6. B	11. D	16. B	21. D	26. A
2. D	7. A	12. D	17. A	22. A	27. D
3. D	8. D	13. A	18. C	23. B	28. D
4. A	9. D	14. D	19. A	24. B	29. C
5. C	10. B	15. C	20. D	25. B	30. C

Short Answer

1. Spontaneous remission and the placebo effect.

2. Chiropractic treatment, acupuncture, naturopathy, herbalists, homeopathy.

3. Largest problem is supply of providers and facilities and your health status.

4. Public administration, nonprofit, comprehensive, universality, accessibility and portability.

Multiple Choice

1. C	6. C	11. D	16. B	21. C	26. D
2. D	7. C	12. A	17. C	22. B	27. B
3. C	8. D	13. B	18. D	23. B	28. B
4. D	9. B	14. B	19. A	24. B	29. A
5. A	10. D	15. B	20. B	25. B	30. B